Because He

By Kathryn L. Thompson

Contents

Dedication

It is my honor to dedicate this book in loving memory of my Grandma (Alma) Geist. It is hard to believe she will never read these words. But she walked with me and my boys through every trial we encountered along the way. We are so thankful for every prayer she prayed on our behalf.

Preface

I am by no means an author. I simply wanted to share my story in hopes that you, the reader, might be helped.

Perhaps you have never walked through divorce, but someone you love has done so. If you have walked through this painful journey, my heart breaks for you. Together, our stories become a part of us and change us into who we are today.

Thank you for sharing in my journey. It is my hope and desire that I have journeyed well. It is not over by any stretch, but I'm thankful we are not alone. I want to offer special thanks to each one who walked with my two boys and me. For those who began the journey with us: My family, Mom, Dad and my sister, Susan. Thank you for loving me and doing all you could to help the boys and I have a new beginning. Thank you for believing in us! A shout out also to W3CU, to Pastor Dan and Cheryl Harrison for praying and giving such comfort in those early moments, to a host of other friends who have given sacrificially behind the scenes, to Nikki Whalen who supported me not just legally but emotionally as well. I can never repay all you have blessed me with.

To Dr Patrick Ward for the gift of mental health and leading us on our journey toward healing. My boys and I will be forever in your debt. To the FBCW church family who have cheered us along on this half of our journey. Special thank you to Mark Musser for your editing expertise. Most importantly I want to thank Jesus. Without His precious gift of forgiveness, I would reside in Hell. I am not perfect, but I am forgiven. He never left our side, not for a single moment in time. May all glory be given to Him. To my sons, Samuel and Josiah, I pray I have loved and led you well. I have been far from perfect in this journey, but you've given grace and love beyond measure. You are my joy, and I am so very blessed that God chose me to be your Mom. You have my heart, and I am so very proud of the young men you are becoming. I have loved every minute of watching you grow in Him, and I look forward to many more.

Introduction

Type…Delete…Type…Delete…Repeat.

That is how this "book" started. It became more therapeutic as I continued to write. I didn't begin with a computer, but with pen and paper. Writing at home, then in a hotel room for an entire month. It is my story. In some cases, peoples names have been changed to protect the privacy of the individuals involved. However, the facts of what happened and the underlying principles have been conveyed as accurately as possible. This story, not one of my own choosing mind you, is far from glamorous. But it is my story.

However, looking back on every event, I wouldn't trade this story for the world. It has molded my boys and me into who we are today. Through it, we have become stronger, braver, and more confident. Not in our own selves but in the One who has walked every step with us.

Chapter One

There are still days I wonder how I got here. This was not God's plan. But in the midst of the mess, He taught me to dream again. He taught Samuel, Josiah and I how to laugh, and how to plan-ahead. I am not the same person I was back in December, 2010. And, really, I never want to be that person again. I am not defined by the sins of another. No, in fact, the Lord has used the sins of another to make me stronger than I ever have been.

I continue to learn every day that God is God and I am not! He has equipped me to parent and raise my boys in such a way that pleases Him. They

belong to Him, and as much as I think no one could care for them like I do, He loves them more than I could imagine. He is a gracious and most patient God. I've learned the hard lesson of leaning on Him to be my everything, in all things. I can have no reservations. He was there when everything around us crumbled, and He showed Himself to be our El Roi, the "God who sees." Nothing that you will read caught Him by surprise.

In the midst of chaos and uncertainty, He was peace. He was our Jehovah-raah, "The Lord Our Shepherd." He cared and met all of our needs. He was constant. I couldn't control things any more than I could control the color of the sky, but God was always, most definitely, in control.

In 2013, if you would have quoted Romans 8:28 to me, I may have slapped you. Really Christian, I know. The world the boys and I had known lay in complete ruin. How could I even begin to see good come out of this nightmare? "And we know (how could I know) that all (even this?) things work together for good to those who love God, (I loved God but how could He allow this to happen) to those called according to His purpose." I couldn't even begin to understand how all of these broken pieces would work together.

The boys and I were devastated. Nothing could have prepared us for what we would face. Yet, this book is a clear testament of the Lord's provision and care for us as we walked through a difficult time.

Chapter Two

In the Beginning…

August 5, 2000, I married my best friend, James Thompson. We had known each other for five years. We fell in love when he was a senior, and I a junior in Bible College. That summer, after his graduation, I went to El Paso, Texas. He went to Iowa, as we both were working on our internships for school.

We began writing letters back and forth. (A fallen art I might add.) My boys find this hilarious because they cannot understand why we wouldn't just talk or text on a cell phone. When I explained that few people owned cell phones back in the "dark ages" of the 1990s, all I received were blank stares. Facebook and Instagram did not exist. Gasp! Truly Mom and Dad are ancient.

Occasionally, we would talk on the phone. Mainly, however, we wrote letters. Hundreds and hundreds. I kept every one--and filled a three-inch binder over time. Unfortunately, the letters would be consumed by termites in storage.

That summer, I was chosen to serve out my internship at a Church of the Nazarene in El Paso, Texas. I would be working with twelve to fourteen teenagers, planning events, speaking weekly at Bible Studies, and even going into Mexico for a short mission trip to serve in an orphanage. I would work directly under the leadership of the senior pastor and keep a strict account of everything done for college credit.

During that time, being 1,700 miles from home, I learned I was capable of so much more. I loved every part of that time. That summer, working with those teens, I grew so much. Having the opportunity to see them grow in their relationship with the Lord right before my eyes was such a privilege.

When I returned to college, in Kentucky, after that summer, I knew I had grown in so many ways. Spiritually, I had matured and my relationship with the Lord had deepened. I would begin my senior year with more passion and focus than all of my other semesters combined.

By October, James and I had "officially" begun to date. Dating at our college was taken very seriously. You had to send a formal request to announce you were in a relationship. With each date more paperwork would need to be filed. You were allowed one on campus date a month…and absolutely no physical touch.

If James and I had to be honest, our feelings for one another began much sooner. But declaring them took a little longer. Every month he would drive ten hours one way from Mississippi where he was attending Wesley Biblical Seminary to visit me, where I was attending college. Life was so different for him. He was living on his own in a dorm owned by the seminary away from the actual campus itself. He was working part-time while going to seminary full-time. He would often tell me I had no idea what real life was all about. I remember becoming so frustrated because he had no sympathy for my anxiousness about an upcoming test. He was barely getting enough hours of sleep with work and school, so his empathy ran thin.

With him so far away, we spent a lot of time on the phone. For me that meant a pay phone in the girls' dorm hallway. Remember phone cards? You paid ten dollars for something like sixty minutes. Well, you could have wallpapered my dorm room with all of mine. I could have supported a small country with what we spent on those ridiculous cards. But you make sacrifices in relationships, especially long distance ones.

Within those sacrifices are many great memories. Like the time James was rearranging his room while we were on the phone. I was having a difficult time and was quiet most of the conversation. Halfway through the conversation, we get disconnected. I kept trying to call back, but the line was busy. He never noticed, and there was no dial tone because he had accidently unplugged it. He begins to pray for me; all the while not noticing I am no longer on the line. When he finally realizes what has happened, I am already in bed asleep. None of his seminary friends let him live that down!

By Thanksgiving, we were spending the holidays with my family in West Virginia. We went for a walk along the Levee in Marietta, Ohio just across the river from where I lived. When we arrived at a gazebo, James got down on one knee and proposed to me. He had already asked my parents' permission earlier that day. When I returned to college following the holiday break, there was no hiding my new status as fiancé. Engagement and wedding rings were the only jewelry allowed. Everyone would know when they saw my ring.

Over Christmas break, I flew down to Mississippi. James had been pastoring a church in a small town called Terry for about six months. It was so exciting to meet those who would become my church family. And they were a wonderful group of people, and we fell in love serving alongside of them.

Chapter Three

After our wedding, in August 2000, a brand new life began for me. James would remain a full-time student while working part-time for the church. I would begin work that September at Union Planters Bank in their loan office.

Several months later, in March, I began to experience a lot of pain. Doctors soon discovered it was my gallbladder. I was scheduled for surgery, but the night before I received a call from a surgical nurse. She was calling to tell me my procedure had been cancelled. My pregnancy test came back positive. We were expecting our first born, whom we would name Samuel.

Four months into my pregnancy, we felt like the Lord was leading us away from the church in Terry. We began to attend a new church plant, called Dayspring, that was then meeting in a roller rink. One of James's professors, Matt Friedeman, pastored there. Many couples from the seminary were attending and that made the transition so much easier. For the first time, we experienced small groups and accountability. And, for the first time, we began to form lasting friendships with other seminary couples. Many of the guys shared classes together, so the wives shared many of the same struggles of having husbands working full-time and attending classes as well.

Our small group leader had an evening class with James taking place at the same time as my Lamaze class, so his wife graciously volunteered to attend it with me. Along with James, she became my labor and delivery coach. Both were there when Samuel arrived that December, eight days before Christmas. Thankfully, my mom flew down three days later to help me with Samuel that first week. She celebrated with us that Christmas, her first away from my dad in thirty years.

After my maternity leave ended, I found out that Union Planters was relocating to Memphis, but I had to be present in the office for the next two weeks in order to receive my severance package. All of our work had already been sent to the new location, so they graciously allowed me to bring Samuel into the office each day. He would have plenty of people loving on him in an office of over two hundred.

After those two weeks, I could finally be a stay at home mom. During this transition, we felt the Lord calling us to pastor a Nazarene Church in Crystal Springs—a small town south of Jackson. God again had given us a great church family. It was a predominately white congregation in a town with an eighty percent African American population.

In September 2002, a friend from college, named Adam, came to work for us in the children's ministry. He lived in the church basement and used our bathroom to shower. At the time, a student from the seminary would bring five African American boys from Jackson to worship with us each Sunday. Generally, they would come over for lunch after church, and we would teach them how to play board games. It was such a joy to be a part of their lives and have the chance to love on them.

We poured everything into that body of believers, and yet our hearts were grieved when the congregation wanted to keep the church segregated. Such a decision began to tear apart the church piece by piece. Moreover, during our time there, I discovered I was pregnant again. At eight months along in my pregnancy, the situation in the church became more serious. Because of the dissention within the church, our salary had been cut to $200 a week. We were unable to fully support ourselves on such an income.

Soon afterwards, my mom and sister arrived, and we began the painful process of resigning from the church and packing up our belongings. I would leave Mississippi entirely and stay with my parents in West Virginia, while James finished his remaining days at the church and completed his final semester at the seminary.

Needless to say, we were devastated. My due date for Josiah was rapidly approaching, and I was six-hundred miles away from my husband! Fortunately, James was able to make it to West Virginia in time. On a chilly Sunday in October, I checked into the hospital for inducement that Monday. Josiah had his own agenda, however, and came that Monday morning at 7:55 am. Five minutes before the procedure was to begin.

James would have to leave Tuesday morning to be on time for his classes on Wednesday. Leaving the hospital that day was so difficult for him--and for me as well. Raising two boys under twenty-two months was so much more difficult than I could imagine. I struggled because I didn't feel like James understood how life was for me. I guess you could compare it to the time I was in college, and he in seminary, when he felt I didn't understand his world of full-time job coupled with a full course load.

Life for me was nursing an infant off and on throughout the night, and then up all day with a two year-old. I was exhausted. A week after Samuel's second birthday in December, James came home. But it proved to be a difficult time for us both. The three month separation had taken its toll. James had one last assignment to complete in order to graduate; it was a two hundred page paper—one he had yet to start writing.

Our first Sunday back home at my parent's church, the pastor called for a spontaneous love offering for my family. The Lord blessed us with one thousand dollars that morning! Meanwhile, my parents were more than gracious to us, opening their home and helping me shoulder the burden while James was away. But when you combine two households under one roof, things can become crowded.

The following year, in January 2004, we began to candidate at several churches. The Lord led us to a church in West Union, Ohio. We began pastoring there that February. Josiah was just four months old, and Samuel was a busy two year-old. The congregation was older, but they loved us and welcomed us into their homes just as if we were family. However, a few months into our ministry there, I began to experience terrible pain, pain that soon became debilitating.

For the next eight months, I truly suffered from excruciating discomfort. During that time, I sought relief from my family practice doctor, a pain specialist, a neurosurgeon, and even a dentist! Finally, the neurosurgeon diagnosed me with Trigeminal Neuralgia-- otherwise known as the "suicide disease." The only relief outside of medication, which I had exhausted, was surgery. It was a very risky surgery due to the location of the nerve involved and the brain stem. It was not a procedure to take lightly. The Sunday before my surgery, the Elders of the church called me forward and anointed my head with oil and laid precious hands on me. I knew God had heard their prayers, for there was this peaceful assurance.

In August of that year, I would undergo the surgery. During the procedure, doctors discovered that I had a nerve wrapped around three blood vessels. With each heartbeat, those blood vessels would pulse resulting in direct pressure on that nerve. Doctors placed a tiny piece of Teflon on the nerve and repositioned the blood vessels. I would spend two days and nights in ICU. The rest of the week would be spent in a step down unit. I became so nauseated after the surgery, I would lose nine pounds in five days. Making it even more difficult for me was the fact that my family and I were all separated during this time. James was preaching at a Camp meeting in Circleville, Ohio, which is located twenty-eight miles south of Columbus, while I was in Riverside Hospital in Columbus itself. Meanwhile, my parents were watching the boys for us in Vienna, West Virginia.

After finally being released into the care of my parents, I was unable to do any lifting for two weeks, and, overall, my recovery would last six weeks. It was hell. I would soon develop migraine headaches accompanied with nausea. These lasted another six months. Our poor church wondered if their pastor's wife would ever emerge, yet they were so gracious and patient with us during this time of healing.

Chapter Four

A few months later, I would be accepted into the RN Nursing Program at Maysville Community College. Maysville, Kentucky was located nineteen miles south of our home in West Union. The weight of it all was greater than I imagined. It was an accelerated program designed to get you through a four year program in two years. At the beginning of the first semester, we were told to bring a picture of our family because that would be all we saw of them. And it was true.

Without James' help, I would not have survived that first year. He cared for the boys and took them on visitations to see the church people. Even when I was home, I was basically locked in my room doing homework. By 2007, after my first (of four) semesters, we felt the Lord calling us to another church. James would join the staff at Winchester Church of Christ in Christian Union as the student life pastor. The transition to this church, fifty-eight miles east of Cincinnati, was difficult. We would be leaving a thriving church that had become our family and home away from home. Looking back, I know this was a crucial step for us to make in our ministry, yet it also meant withdrawing from the nursing program and beginning to work full-time outside the home, working third shift in a nursing home.

It was a hard day going before my advisor and leaving the program I had worked so diligently to get into. I was given the opportunity to return to the program one year later and pick up where I left off, but that would not be possible.

Soon we found a home twenty miles from our new church. This location put us closer to Cincinnati and just ten miles from my job at the nursing home. That summer, and the two to follow, would be difficult, as I sought to juggle working all night then caring for the boys during the day. Josiah began early admission for pre-school due to a speech delay, while Samuel entered Kindergarten. We were able to secure two to three days a week for daycare, so I could get caught up on much needed sleep.

James working so hard at the church, beginning a third service for twenty-something's. We were really beginning to thrive amongst other couples our age. It was a great time in the church. Before long, I was able to transition into another third shift job with benefits. I would be working in a group home for the mentally handicapped. This job opened the door for long lasting friendships, but it was physically and emotionally demanding. During this time, we also began small groups in our home. Our home seemed always full of friends and food! I loved it! Our kids loved it. It was a great time in ministry.

Chapter Five

In June of 2010, I was able to attend the Emmaus Walk. This amazing event is a three day experience where "pilgrims," as you are called while on the "walk," are joined in small groups to support one another in their ongoing walk with Christ. The objective is to inspire, challenge, and equip local church members for Christian action in their homes, churches, communities, and places of work.[i] If you've never had the privilege of attending, please prayerfully consider this life changing opportunity. You will never regret a decision to do so.

On the first day of the walk, I, along with my fellow pilgrims, entered into a dimly lit sanctuary and were led up on the stage. In the pews in front of us were "pilgrims" who had gone on previous walks. They were holding candles and singing together. Out in the crowd, I could see James. After they finished the song, they all filed out of the sanctuary single file. James jumped out of line and ran up on the stage and kissed me. It was amazing. I was so proud of him.

Before my time on the Emmaus Walk would end, I had the privilege of getting to better know those assigned to my table during that weekend. One lady in particular went to our church. Her name was Nikki. She attended the first service and I the third. Still, we had met each other on occasion, most often in the church nursery. With our boys around the same age, she quickly became a friend, and someone I would lean on in the future. I believe God allowed her and I to be at the same table for a special reason.

Later that same year in June, James had led a brief devotional at District Assembly, which was a tremendous privilege. Afterwards, a pastor met with him and offered James and I a few days away at a Condo. It came at the perfect time, as we would be celebrating our tenth wedding anniversary that August. We decided to use this gift in June. It was located right on Lake Erie and the view was spectacular. I had wanted to renew our vows for our anniversary, and we thought maybe we would on this trip. We used these few days away as a chance to talk about my future. James really wanted me to return to nursing school, while I desperately wanted a third child. Every conversation centered on these two decisions.

At night, we slept with the bedroom door open and fell asleep listening to the waves. The day before we were set to come home, it seemed like James and I were no closer to making a decision about my future. Then, that afternoon, we both received a friend request on Facebook from a girl neither of us knew. I declined, while he accepted. That decision would have life-altering consequences for our family. A relationship between James and this woman would span the next six months. A long time later, James would tell me he never wanted another child with me. Looking back, as painful as it was to hear, I know God was protecting me.

Chapter Six

By July 2010, the third shift job had become increasingly stressful. I felt isolated from James and the boys. On top of that, my schedule only allowed me to attend church every fifth Sunday. I put in my two week notice, and the Lord graciously opened the doors for what would be my dream job--a position at the local library. I had a passion for books and what better job could there be than cataloging new ones. It was a part-time position that allowed me the benefit of putting my boys on the bus in the morning and being home when they got off. I would have every weekend off and all holidays. It had been a long four years to get to where I was, and I was over the moon. The position had the potential of becoming full-time upon the retirement of my supervisor in a year. And more importantly, once again, the Lord blessed me with meaningful friendships with the staff.

James was so busy that summer. In seven weeks, he would be a part of five camps across West Virginia, Indiana, Ohio and Kentucky. It felt like he was never home. But when the school year started, things returned to normal pace. The street we lived on had the perfect place for evening walks as a family. It was a winding, mile-long road with a dead end. Nearby sat a lovely little pond where James took the boys fishing a few times.

It was on one of those walks that James told me he had smoked marijuana. He had been home in Kentucky with his family; specifically with his cousins who grew marijuana. I was livid. Wasn't this something you did in college? Surely not something a thirty-something *pastor*, married with two kids, did! For me, there was no justification. He assured me it was a onetime, stupid thing that would never take place again. Still, I was so upset. He was a pastor; someone in a leadership role that could not take things like this lightly.

Something was happening. He was pulling away...or was I pushing him? Either way, things only got worse.

He had also begun to drink. Casually. Never out in public. Only at home. Never beer, usually Vodka. However, it became more than casual when I was working third shift. Having to leave the house at 9:30 pm for several years, I would not know the extent of this habit until much later.

One Friday, in October 2010, there was a knock on the door. I didn't recognize the guy standing on our doorstep, but he quickly introduced himself as Andy from Child Protective Services. What in the world was he doing here? One of the boys had gone to school and told a teacher that his daddy choked him. And this man, Andy, was there to investigate. I clearly explained that the night before had been a rough night with homework. My child had been tired and was crying. James lost his patience, grabbed my child's chin, and told him to calm down. Never, not once, did he place his hands on the neck area at all. And he certainly did not threaten him in any way.

Nevertheless, James wouldn't be allowed back into the home until Monday after he met with a counselor and a sheriff to close the investigation. He had me call James while he was there and explain to him the situation. The following morning we, as a family, were testing for our green senior belts in karate. James would not be allowed at the promotion, even to just watch. After the promotion, the boys and I went to my parent's house until Sunday night. That gave James the opportunity to be in the house and prepare for his message on Sunday.

Looking back at this event, I see more clearly that the lie told by my child that day was very wrong. However, this lie led to James having to leave the house and myself discovering several inconsistencies with James' marijuana story. But I am getting ahead of myself.

The boys returned to school on Monday, and I went into work. While I was there, James called me. He said that if he was drug tested before his interview he would not pass.

Who had he become?

Chapter Seven

I was devastated. I didn't know him anymore. I left work early in tears and went home to pray. Restless, I began doing things around the house. (This is "normal" for me. When I am under stress or simply need to clear my head, I clean.) I decided to begin in the kitchen and straighten it up. While doing so, I noticed the dog needed food in her bowl, so I headed to the garage where her food was kept. Opening the food bag, I saw a sandwich bag containing a few joints. One had already been smoked half-way. I took the bag, and placed it by James' coffee pot with a note asking him, "Why hide it?" I left the house, went to the park, and prayed again.

While I was there, I called a college friend who had been in the dorm with James and knew him well. He was also a pastor, so I trusted his guidance and help. But how does one begin that conversation, even with a friend? It felt like betrayal. Not to mention the humiliation of all this. And what exactly was "this?" What else was he hiding?

My friend's advice was that it was my responsibility to confront James, confront him with the opportunity to come clean or have me come clean for him. I was heartbroken. How did we get here? He was a stranger to me. I wonder now if he even recognized himself when he looked in the mirror.

Summoning up the courage, I did confront James, stating, "You come clean or I will have to do it for you." He adamantly refused to admit anything. Moreover, he threatened me against doing so. The thought that I would even consider it enraged him. About an hour later, I stood there in our church sanctuary, red faced from crying. Grieved and humiliated. The associate pastor saw me first, and we went into his office. He knew the strain I was experiencing in my marriage, as I had been seeing him for counseling for a few weeks. I could barely speak. It all seemed to come out in one breath.

There were no words from him. He left the room and returned with the senior pastor. So many questions swirled in my mind. Would this be it for James and me? Would our marriage survive? Would this be the end of our ministry? What would happen to our boys?

As I shared the struggle in our home, and the painful choice to come forward, they were obviously grieved and disappointed. Most of all, however, they were concerned. They became grace to me that day, refusing to cast a stone. They did not condemn, judge, or even lash out. Instead, the two men stated the obvious. James would be removed from ministry (for an undetermined amount of time), while he met with counselors and followed through on some discipline guidelines set before him. They would do whatever possible to help him return to ministry, to walk in redemption, and to live in complete restoration. Each pastor assured me of their love and commitment to see us *both* through this strenuous time. They would meet with James later that afternoon when he returned from the Sheriffs' department. It all felt so hopeful.

Sadly, the feeling wouldn't last.

The bridge between us was burning, and I had just poured gasoline over it all. James was furious with me when he returned home. Already reeling from a mandatory six weeks of counseling ordered by the Sheriff's Office, he couldn't believe he was now also removed from the pastorate and forced to undergo even more remediation. Though the pastors were gracious to him and had lain out a much disciplined plan for him to be restored into leadership, he was filled with such rage he couldn't see any of it.

Things were definitely spiraling now. At the time, however, I didn't know just how much.

My birthday came a short time later, and James planned to take the family out for lunch. What he forgot to mention was that he would be bringing three youth along. Not really a big deal, except I was really looking to some time with just him and the boys. After lunch, though, he decided he would take the youth to a movie—without us. The boys and I would end up going home alone.

Even though it was only October, setting up the Christmas tree early had been a family tradition since Samuel was two, so we set up the tree without James. And when he still wasn't home by supper, the boys and I made a cake together and put in a movie to watch. The boys were in bed by the time he finally came home. I was so disappointed. He had not even got me a card. He was miserable with me, and I knew it.

In November, the church sent us on a Marriage Counseling retreat. Tucked in the Tennessee Mountains was Fairhaven. A place designed for pastors and Christian workers to get away and recharge. They had a Christian counselor on site who would come to our cabin each day for one and a half hours of counseling. There was no cell phone service, no land line, no TV, not even a radio. Each cabin had a small library, a collection of books set aside for you to enjoy during your stay as well as a few board games.

Preparing to leave for Fairhaven was agonizing. I knew he didn't want to be with me at all, let alone in a cabin with me for a whole week. How would we even survive a six and a half hour car ride? Close friends from church had volunteered to watch the boys for us. Their children attended the same school as ours so that would make things a lot easier for transportation.

Before we left, I received a text from James that he would never be intimate with me again because of my weight. How does one accept something like that and move forward? He also wanted me to know he would not be sharing the same room with me in the cabin. He was furious that we were even going and had to spend this time together. I was devastated. He was the one I had been most vulnerable with. He was mine and I was his. When did it all become a lie? How did I miss my husband falling out of love with me?

Chapter Eight

During our week at Fairhaven, I began journaling. From my journal -- Day One -- *There must be another way. He seems so far from you [God]. How did this happen? My heart is broken. The one I looked to lead our family has fallen. The boys will be devastated. Please let your will be done this week. Release my expectations of what must happen.*

Day Two -- *"Psalm 103: Praise the Lord, O my soul; all my inmost being, praise His holy name. Praise the Lord, O my soul, and forget not all his benefits, who forgives all your sins and heals all your diseases, who redeems your life from the pit and crowns you with love and compassion, who satisfies your desires with good things so that your youth is renewed like the eagles. The Lord works righteousness and justice for all the oppressed. He made known His ways to Moses, His deeds to the people of Israel; the Lord is compassionate and gracious, slow to anger, abounding in love, he will not always accuse, nor will he harbor his anger forever; he does not treat us as our sins deserve or repay us according to our iniquities. For as high as the heavens are above the earth so great is his love for those who fear him as far as the east is from the west, so far has he removed our transgressions from us." [ii]*

Today, as I journaling and praying, I asked God to help me love James where he was hurting and broken. These days are brutal. The counselor has come every day and met with us for over two hours each time. James is continuing to go on and on about his relationship with his dad. I feel like he is wasting time. We are not here because of his relationship with his dad! The counselor continues to interrupt him and redirect him as to why we are really here--but still nothing changes. James shares his idea that perhaps there is a denomination that will accept his new "habits." What? Habits? We could not continue this way, especially serving in ministry.

Day Four -- *I begin reading and writing out Psalm 116 and ask God to help my doubts and help me to stand on his promises. James reveals today that he has never found me attractive and continues the argument with, "Look at her, she is obese." Thankfully, the counselor stops him. I feel like everything is crumbling. How was it possible that he never loved me? I ask God to heal me and redeem what has been broken. I ask for his help to identify who I am in him. "In all this, help me to love."*

39

Each day the counselor encouraged us to leave the property and allow for some time apart. I wonder now if the counselor felt like a conductor on a runaway train, frantically working to keep the train from total destruction. I called every day to check in on the boys, spoke with my mom, and called a friend. I felt so broken. My spirit was crushed. It seemed surreal. James wouldn't talk to me at all. The cabin was very quiet. You could hear a pin drop, or an ant crawl across the floor. It was as if I was the enemy.

Day Five – *I've lost who I am. I've lost my sense of value and worth.*

Let me jump in here a second and explain. For our whole marriage, James had been on a pedestal for me. I had a relationship with the Lord. Yet, on many levels, it was shallower than I ever knew. I allowed myself to be defined by another person and for that I opened the door to always feel "less than." I didn't know who I was without him. I was never an equal with him. He made most of the decisions, and I allowed him to do so with generally no argument. I never knew the state of our finances other than what he told me or allowed me to know.

I have learned so much about myself since that day. Frankly, I am embarrassed it took so long. I begged God while we were still in Tennessee to show me again and again who I was in Him. No longer would I allow another human being to define me. I further begged God to forgive James. I desperately wanted restoration in our relationship, but it just seemed to be slipping away. I asked the Lord to give understanding to the boys. For, in Him, they needed a faith that would stand strong no matter what happened.

Day Six -- *I am angry God. I am hurting. I am angry at James. But more so, I am angry with myself. How did I not see this coming? I am angry because ten years of my life seem gone. What I've valued and held dear were all lies. I'm angry because I don't feel like You were there for me. I'm hurt because he rejected me. Each day only confirms that he never loved me. He repeats it again and again. Almost to make sure I understand that he no longer wants me or this marriage. Even the counselor is frustrated.*

Our last night there we talk, for the first time, about the next few weeks. How will we celebrate Thanksgiving? We have always celebrated together with his family at

Thanksgiving and with mine at Christmas. He tells me I can take the boys to West Virginia, and he will go alone to his family in Kentucky. We decide together that now might be the best time to do Christmas shopping for the boys because we are unsure how things will be then. So, there we were in *Toys R Us* in Johnson City, Tennessee, standing in the toy aisle. I was already crying, and he was on his phone. It became an agonizing process. This was supposed to be a joyful time for families, yet I was an emotional wreck, and he was absent from any involvement. We purchased wrapping paper, and I wrapped the presents in silence at the cabin later that night.

When we arrived home later the next day, we greeted the boys. In minutes, he retreated to the man cave. Before Thanksgiving, he took an overnight trip to Louisville and decided while he is there he would just stay another day, ignoring the fact that the extra day was Sunday and he was supposed to be at our church. Needless to say this was problematic. (I didn't know then, but he was not alone on that trip.)

Thanksgiving was there before I knew it, and the boys and I headed to my parents "to celebrate." But my parents knew. They could see it on my face before I even said anything--things were not well. I sat down with each of them and confessed that my marriage might not survive. The news devastated.

To help me out any way they possibly could, my parents sent me back to Ohio with some cash because James withheld money from me. With the money my parents gave to me, I bought groceries and simply hung onto the rest. December came. You could feel the tension in our home. It seemed I could do little right to please James. Work was hard. Even though the job was fairly easy, I felt so far away emotionally and mentally.

Before long, he moved out of our room and slept in his man cave on a love seat. Wherever he went, his cell phone followed. They were tethered together at all times. If he was taking a shower, the phone was with him and the door locked. December 17th arrived and with it Samuel's birthday. We celebrated with friends at *Chuck E Cheese*. Even our friends commented to me about James' behavior. He clearly was absent, only physically present. He had become distant even amongst friends. He was so far from all of us.

Christmas Eve morning came, and we were opening our presents early because we would be spending Christmas Eve at my parents. The boys were already sitting around the tree when I went to get James out of his man cave. I explained we were ready to celebrate. He responded with, "Let's hurry up and get this over with." The boys never knew how painful that time was around the tree was for me, and for that I am grateful.

Earlier on Christmas Eve, I woke early and had my morning devotions at the table. I felt the Lord leading me to a passage in Isaiah 54 beginning in verse 4:

> "Do not be afraid; you will not suffer shame. Do not fear disgrace; you will not be humiliated...for your Maker is your husband-the Lord Almighty is His name-the Holy One of Israel is your Redeemer; he is called the God of all the earth. The Lord will call you back as if you were a wife deserted and distressed in spirit-a wife who married young, only to be rejected," says your God.

> "For a brief moment I abandoned you. But with deep compassion I will bring you back. In a surge of anger I hid my face from you for a moment, but with everlasting kindness I will compassion on you," says the Lord your Redeemer...Though the mountains be shaken and the hills removed, yet my unfailing love for you will not be shaken nor my covenant of peace removed," says the Lord, who has compassion on you.

44

"O afflicted city, lashed by storms and not comforted. I will build you with stones of turquoise, your foundations with sapphires I will make your battlements of rubies, your gates of sparkling jewels, and all your walls of precious stones. All your sons will be taught by the Lord, and great will be your children's peace. In righteousness you will be established: Tyranny will be far from you; you will have nothing to fear. Terror will be far removed; it will not come near you. If anyone does attack you, it will not be my doing; whoever attacks you will surrender to you...no weapon forged against you will prevail, and you will refute every tongue that accuses you. This is the heritage of the servants of the Lord, and this is their vindication from me," declares the Lord."[iii]

Being led to those verses felt so strange because it wasn't a passage for Advent, and I didn't understand its meaning. Yet, somehow, I knew it was meant for me. (I wouldn't discover until later how much that passage of Scripture would mean.) That afternoon, we left for my parents' house. We arrived in time to attend their church's Christmas Eve Service. James was miserable, and everyone noticed. Christmas morning was no different. He left to answer his phone while we were exchanging presents. Clearly, he couldn't wait to get away.

We had previously made arrangements for the boys to spend a few days with my parents on their Christmas break because I would be working. James came into my parents' kitchen and asked if we could leave early and head to his family's house to celebrate. Of course, my family was hurt because he had practically ignored them, opened his presents, and wanted nothing more than to leave early.

Nevertheless, soon we were on the road again in order to make it to James' family before nightfall. However, then James decided that we should go home first and just leave early the next morning. That night he told me he would rather go alone, since I never really enjoyed going there in the first place. I was so hurt. I could have stayed with my parents for another day, but he had wanted to leave early. I laid in bed and cried. Finally, he decided we should go together, so we left the next morning. Arriving at his family's house to celebrate Christmas felt so fake. His family acted very strange toward me, while James ignored me completely. Eventually, one of his cousins, Justin, asked me how we were doing, and I said I didn't know. Nothing could have been more honest. Justin would tell me that he didn't understand James anymore. Someone he had always looked up to was a stranger to him as well. But Justin was one in whom I had grown close to in the family. So his opinion mattered a great to me. Justin had also attended college together with James and I. James was well-respected within his family, often taking opportunities to preach at his mother's church each time we visited. He was the apple of his grandfather's eye. He was very proud of him. His grandfather had made a huge investment into his life as a young Christian. He was so proud of James serving in ministry.

On our way home, later that night, we were in a restaurant. I asked him if he had ever been unfaithful to me. He smirked, then got up from the table to go use the restroom. Who doesn't answer a question like that?!?

I was on pins and needles awaiting an answer. Yet, none came. And when we arrived home, he acted as though all was right with the world.

Chapter Nine

There are days in our lives that will never leave us. Specific dates burned into our memories. Without thinking, we can clearly recall where we were and what we were doing. For me, December 28, 2010, is one of those days.

At about 2:00 pm on that day, James showed up at the library wearing a suit jacket. All dressed up, he asked if there was any way I could leave work early because he wanted to take me out on a date. I checked with my boss, and she said it was fine. We headed to Cincinnati to catch a movie. Afterwards, we went to Olive Garden because it was my favorite restaurant. Our hostess sat us in the center of the restaurant at a table just for two.

As we were ordering our meal, James asked if he could get an alcoholic drink. He had never ordered alcohol out in public before, so this was something new. Looking back on this, how I wish I would have spoken up and said, "No." I didn't approve that alcohol had become such a part of his life. As we were waiting for our meal to arrive, James passed a small white box to me. Inside sat a gorgeous Amethyst necklace with matching earrings; very expensive, and completely out of the ordinary. We didn't have the money for such gifts, and this was the first time James had bought me jewelry outside of our wedding bands and engagement ring. It certainly was a gesture that should have hit me as a red flag!

I thanked him, then pushed it aside as our meal had arrived. We ate quietly. Then, just as I finished, he said there was something he needed to tell me. I was all ears. "Well, you ought to know by now that I've been unfaithful."

My mouth went dry. I couldn't form any words. I simply stared at him, while he continued without missing a beat.

James shared that one of his affairs was with a woman he met online. "That was a one-time thing," he said, "That's over."

But there was a second one as well…with Jessica.

It was as if all the air left the room. There we sat in the very center of that restaurant surrounded by people at every corner. Jessica! I knew Jessica! She was one of the youth in our church! This teen had been in our home many times over the previous few months because she came from a troubled home, and we were trying to mentor her. She and I had even baked cookies together.

I racked my brain searching for answers. The two of them were never alone at our house. When and how did this happen? My heart was breaking. Sitting there, I began to sob. I threw the necklace in my purse and left the table in tears. I barely made it to the parking lot before I vomited. Sitting in the middle of the parking lot, tears streamed down my cheeks feeling completely humiliated. It took me nearly twenty minutes to compose myself enough to call up a close friend from college.

After I explained as best I could what had taken place, she and her husband extended an invitation for me to stay with them at her parent's home for a few days. I certainly needed a place to go and gather my thoughts, a place to try to make sense of all that had just happened.

Nearly an hour had passed before James finally emerged from the restaurant. I cried most of the way home when I wasn't asking questions. Well, to be honest, I only asked two. The first was if he had given that youth a card for her birthday. He answered, "Yes." Why that even mattered to me under the circumstances I cannot remember, except that on my birthday I received nothing from him. The second question was if she was sixteen when their affair began. Again, he answered, "Yes." I couldn't ask anymore.

When we arrived home, I needed to get away from him, so I went out driving. I didn't get very far because I found myself pulling into the library where I had been working. I went inside to see if my manager was on that night. I knew I would need a few days off to sort through everything. She was there, and we went into her office. I sat there and couldn't believe what I was about to say, "My husband has been unfaithful; and I think I may need a few days off."

Nothing about saying that felt real. She quickly came from across her desk and sat next to me, wrapping me in a big hug. She assured me that whatever time I needed off would not be a problem. Little did I know then that I would not return for five days and then only to hand in my resignation and to say goodbye. The library was one of my favorite places, and everyone had been so welcoming to me. Closing that door was so very hard.

When I arrived home, I went directly to our bedroom to pack. He was furious with me. "You cannot tell the church now. We have to wait until May," he screamed.

It was December, and there was no way I could withhold this from them for that long. It wasn't even an option for me. His reason behind "the plan" was so that we could be farther out of debt before we left the church. The rest of "the plan" was that I would leave my part time job and get a full-time job that paid more. I swore at him; only once. Still not justified, I know. I explained to him that I was not the one with all the extra time on my hands and, therefore, would not be leaving my job.

About an hour later, I met with friends to get away. Samuel and Josiah were still with my parents in West Virginia for a few more days until school restarted. My friend's parents were gracious to open their home to me during this time. I stayed with them for three days and two nights. Their home became my haven.

Grief seemed to come in waves. It all felt like a horrible nightmare. I had so many questions. What was my role now? Where do we go from here? Could I forgive? Would he change? What would happen to the boys? My friends listened, while I wrestled with each question, and they held me when all I could do was cry.

The night before I left, this wonderful family gathered around the piano to sing, not the Christmas songs that we all had grown tired of, but worship songs. I remember distinctly trying to hang onto every word of "How Great is Our God."

He wraps himself in light and darkness tries to hide and trembles at His voice. How great is our God. Sing with me, how great is our God and all will see how great, how great is our God.[iv]

But I could hold on no longer. It felt like Darkness had won. Defeat was all I could accept. I went into my room and simply cried out to God. Not pretty tears, and not well-thought out prayers, only pleading sobs. It was all just pure, raw, unforgiving emotion.

As cathartic as that time had been, I knew it couldn't last. The boys would be coming home that Friday, and James and I still had so much to work through. Was it even possible to do so? Still, I was committed to doing whatever was possible to make our marriage work. Later, when James picked me up from that blessed haven, I told him I was committed to him and our marriage, but it was not an option to withhold his struggles from the pastors or the church any longer. He agreed to that with one change. He would only admit to one of the affairs. No, I wouldn't agree to that. They deserved to know it all.

Once we arrived back home, I walked through the front door, put my bags down, and there right in front of me, on the couch, lay a pair of jeans. I went straight for them. Picking them up, I could see that they were size-2. Clearly not my jeans. I calmly asked James who they belonged to, and he told me they were Jessica's. He went on to explain that he had brought her over to the house to end it while I was gone.

"And she left her pants?" I picked them up, threw them at his face, and told him to leave the house. He just stood there; so I restated everything—this time screaming. He left. I fell down and sobbed. How can one person fight to save their marriage when the other will not chose to be faithful? How could everything keep crumbling before we could even begin to salvage anything?

After calling a friend, I knew I needed to speak next with the senior pastor. However, it was New Year's Eve, and he had family in from out of town to celebrate the holidays. This news would ruin everything for them. But I knew I had to do it. That was the most difficult phone call I ever made in my life. How do you even begin that conversation? Admitting complete defeat? He answered the phone that night at 11:00 pm, and he felt the devastation and shock right along with me. He was broken for James, grieved at the choices he had made in spite of all their efforts to help him move toward restoration.

He offered to bring his wife over, so they could be there with me. I felt confident that I was safe and would be okay. So we arranged to meet the following day, after I had gotten the boys from my parents. I hung up the phone in a virtual state of shock.

Much too upset to sleep, and without the ability to carry on an intelligent conversation on the phone, I did what I do best. I cleaned. I went into my bedroom and saw the bed was unmade and the room a mess. Someone had gone through my closet, dresser and jewelry box. My Christmas gift, and amethyst necklace, were missing. I shut the door and didn't go back in there for over a week.

Seeking white noise, I searched for the TV remote control, yet I couldn't find it anywhere. Having looked everywhere else, I went into James' man cave and discovered a bag with gifts inside. He had purchased

Jessica the same gifts he had given me for Christmas. Disgusted, I got down on the floor, still looking for the remote. Under the bookcases, I noticed something, only it wasn't the remote. No, it was James' black journal.

James had journaled his entire life. And, before this time, I had never read any of his entries unless there was something he wanted to show me. But, now, everything had changed. It was time to see what had been going on in my husband's head. So I opened it up, and for the next two hours, I read it from cover to cover. The content was heavy, dark and tragic. It read like a chronicle of sins. Sins against him, the boys, our church, and me. I began at the back--I am still not sure why--and immediately felt like I was reading the journal of someone I didn't know.

October 27, 2010 -- *where do I begin? For two months now I have been in a relationship with Jessica. I honestly have never been happier than when I am alone with her. She has made specific demands, however, insisting that I completely reject Kathy and refuse her all affections, which I have done. I told Kathy I was unhappy with our marriage and I wanted out. Kathy went to the pastors about smoking pot and they confronted me. They are removing me from any ministry roles for two months. They are sending us to a counseling retreat Fairhaven. Jessica will not stand for any of this. Once she hears that Kathy and I are leaving for a week together she will never speak to me again. I will grieve her loss like no other. No one has ever made me so happy. What I want is to run away with Jessica...but it so much easier said than done.*

I continued to read, but it didn't feel real. I became sick. I had been living with a complete stranger for years. I couldn't even comprehend how long this had been his reality. After I finished the journal, I felt completely void of any emotion. It was just too much to comprehend. I went into the living room and lay down on the couch with the journal under me. About thirty minutes later, I heard the door unlock. James walked in, went straight to his man cave, and locked the door, refusing to leave.

At four in the morning, I quickly and quietly dressed, then headed Jackson, Ohio. It was eighty miles away, a relatively short drive to get my boys. I was nearly four hours early to meet my mom, but resting in the car somehow felt safer.

Chapter Ten

My mom and the boys meet me at a Bob Evans, in Jackson, Ohio around 9:00 am. It felt so good to see the boys after such a long break apart. They had a wonderful time hanging out at my parent's house in West Virginia, but they were ready to return home. Yet, what would "home" look like for them? How would I explain where their dad had gone? My mom gave me some money again to help with anything I might need over the next few days.

Before we left, I called the senior pastor and told him the contents of the journal. He was just as furious as I was. James had lied about everything. His confession was nothing but a joke. What he had done was serious. Criminal in fact. A Class 3 Felony in the state of Ohio. As the boys and I left Jackson, I called a good friend who opened her home to us to just crash until the afternoon when we met with the senior pastor and his wife.

As we waited, the boys asked where Daddy was, and I had no idea what to tell them. We left our friend's house and grabbed pizza for supper. They were only six and eight, so small to be going through all this. As I gazed into their innocent faces, it hit me. They had no idea how much their world would be changing.

The senior pastor and his wife, Dan and Cheryl, met me in the main office to go over the contents of the journal. Dan discussed his responsibility to the church and to the state. Charges would have to be pressed. In the end, I gave the journal to Dan to keep safe. I would never read it again. Eventually, two years later, I would give my copy to my counselor because it had become a temptation to read. Reading it again would only prevented me from moving on. It actually proved to be very helpful for my counselor to understand James better by reading it. He called it the "Diary of a Mad Man."

After I left the church that night, the boys and I got home at around nine in the evening. We were all so tired that we quickly got ready for bed. I slept with them in their room with the door locked. James would message later that he was in Louisville that night. He wanted me to know that if I came across a black journal of his to not read it but to burn it. However, it was now too late for self-preservation.

I cannot even recall what we did on Saturday, but on Sunday we went to church, just the three of us. My parents were planning on coming in that afternoon to help me with whatever was needed. Being in the service that morning felt surreal. Other than a time or two of being sick, there had never been a time when we were not all in service together. (With the exception of when I worked third shift and only had off every fifth Sunday.) I do not remember a song we sang or the title of the message. I simply remember the people. Each one had become a part of our family. We laughed together, cried together and always found a reason to celebrate something together. They, too, would experience all the emotions we were experiencing. Our home, our family, our friends and our church would never be the same again.

When my parents and sister arrived later that day, my mother gathered my bedroom linens and threw them away. She then went out and purchased new sheets and straightened up the room. Later that afternoon, there was a knock on the front door. It was my mother- in-law, Anna. She came inside like we had been there waiting for her arrival. The reality was I had no idea what she was doing there. She hadn't called; she simply showed up.

As she came in the door she hugged me and whispered in my ear "I don't see why you can't just forgive him. You kicked him out of this house!"

Did I misunderstand her? What right did she have to come into my home and speak to me in such a way? Before I could process any of this, she went right over and plopped herself down at the dining room table where we had just sat down for supper a few moments earlier. I was still struggling to process it all when I received a text message from James. He had called the Sheriff, and I had to leave the property within the hour or be removed. He wanted to come and get his dresser and TV.

I hastily gathered some clothes for the boys and me, along with some valuables. I wasn't sure what to do or where to go, so I called Dan. He invited my family right over. None of us understood what James was doing or what he would do next. While we were at Pastor Dan's, he made a phone call on my behalf to an attorney. He was able to secure me an 8:00 am appointment for Monday morning with Nikki. Yes, the same Nikki who sat at my table on the Emmaus Walk. She gave me a card that weekend. Inside it, she had written, *I look forward to getting to know you better.* I am certain that this was not what she had in mind!

Cheryl went with me to the appointment to help with any questions and to make sense of what instructions we were given. I am so thankful she came with me that day. I would have been a mess without her there. We arrived at Nikki's office and it was only then I realized I had not put on any socks that cold morning. It was January after all.

As I took a seat in the office, I could barely think how to begin the conversation. Nikki encouraged me to begin at the beginning and take what time I needed. I began with "James has been unfaithful..." She was professional, but you could see that her heart broke with mine. He was her pastor as well.

Soon we got down to details. I needed to know about our finances—what was our debt? What did we own? Whose name was on the house? And so much more. James took care of all of that, but together we would need to go over everything on the home computer.

As if all of that wasn't mind-blowing enough, Nikki moved next to explain the steps to divorce...wait, what?

Divorce hadn't even entered my mind. We couldn't divorce, could we? Cheryl asked appropriate questions and took pages of notes for me. Before leaving, Nikki introduced us to a few girls from her office. They were so compassionate. The following Christmas, I would receive a beautiful card and a check from those office girls. The card read, "We hope this makes your Christmas a little easier..." and it did.

When we left her office, we went directly to Pastor Dan's office where we discussed everything. The word *divorce* had hit all of us hard. I took all of the notes home and gave them to my sister. She had offered her help and was always great with making sense of paperwork, so I turned it all over to her. Without internet in the house, I then left for a friend's place of business to print off our bank statements. It proved to be more difficult than we imagined. Everything was password protected and guidelines were set for how many previous months you could retrieve your bank statements. Finally, after a lot of work, we were able to print them, but they were not making sense to me. Hotel charges? Room service? Valet parking? Restaurants and movies? Party stores and alcohol? None of it made sense at all. I could barely even cry; I just felt numb...and humiliated.

None of these charges were on our home computer; I would have seen them before. I gathered the statements together and headed back to the house where I met my sister. She had even more difficult news. She found two letters from our mortgage company that stated we were more than seven months behind in payment. In fact, we were behind on every bill (electric, water, sewage etc.) except our cell phone bill. And, on that bill, another phone had recently been added. We were paying for Jessica's cell phone. The weight of all this seemed too overwhelming to be true.

Soon people, some I had never met before, were gathered in my home to pack it up. It was really happening. The boys and I were moving out. I guess, in my mind, I thought I could live in the house with the boys. But that was not possible, especially with almost every account so far behind in payment. Frankly, it was God's blessing that none of the utilities had been shut off.

Chapter Eleven

It didn't take long for Pastor Dan to contact James about charges being pressed, and he quickly began texting, blaming me for it all. The texts stated that he didn't deserve my rage, and I was only seeking revenge by going to the pastors. Indeed, life was never going to be the same.

The boys returned to class on Tuesday morning after the holiday break was over. My dad and I went directly to the school that morning to let them know some of what was happening. They agreed to call us should James come and request the boys leave with him. Meanwhile, the principle spoke with the boys' teachers and explained to them the circumstances should there be any problems.

From there, Dad and I went to the bank to open a new checking account for me so that the last of my checks could be deposited somewhere safe. My mind felt like mush. They asked for my address, and I couldn't remember it. If my dad had not been there, I'm not sure what I would have done. When the boys returned from school, my father took us all out for supper and then we made a run to Sam's club to purchase plastic and bubble wrap. We needed to begin the packing process.

Trying to do all we could to make the transition as easy for the boys as possible, we bought them each cupcakes to take to school the next day. It would be their last day. That night, once we got home, I sat the boys down on the couch. Sitting in front of them on the floor, I told them we were moving to West Virginia. I explained that Daddy would not be able to come with us, and they soon questioned why. Again, they were only six and eight at the time. I knew I could never tell them the details at that age, if ever. Finally, Samuel asked if Daddy had sinned. I kept my response to a simple, "Yes," and assured them that they would be okay and safe. The next day, they would board their school bus for the last time, cupcakes in hand.

The following morning, I woke up early. To be honest, I'm not sure if I ever even went to sleep that night. There I sat at what was once *our* dining room table and tried to understand what had taken place. Right in front of me was a house in shambles--even the Christmas tree was still up, since it was just a few days into the New Year. How could I move in just two days with nothing packed?

Two cherished friends came over that morning to do all they could to help my mom and sister get the house packed as quickly as possible. Meanwhile, my dad was out running errands and securing a U-Haul truck for the trip home.

Meanwhile, I was handling other matters, as I actually was called into the Sheriffs' Department to give my testimony. Pastor Dan met me there and, although he wasn't allowed in the room with me, I felt his support and prayers from the waiting room.

Pastor Dan had graciously made me two copies of the journal in its entirety. For my meeting, I brought just a few of the pages from it--the ones regarding the affair with a minor. The detective that was working on James' case was the same one who had worked on the Child Protective Services case a few months prior. The detective, named Carl, was kind, compassionate and knew how painful this interview would be for me. As it was being recorded, all I could think of was how James would only see this as a "revenge move" on my part.

I began at the beginning, and he listened without interrupting me. Then he asked for the journal, and I gave him the copies. After reviewing them, he carefully explained that it would not be enough. He needed the original and went on to further explain they could issue a search warrant and that would mean a lot of police at our house looking for this journal. That was when I told him that I had it in the car, so we walked outside to retrieve it. After handing it to him, I asked if there was any way we could only use the parts dealing with Jessica and not submit the journal in its entirety. That, he stated, would be left up to the prosecutor.

I asked what to do next. He gave me two things: File for divorce and move out. I explained my plan to move on Friday, to which he replied, "You must move now because when a story like this hits the media; your kids will pay a high price, and everyone will know."

From the Sheriffs' Department, I headed to my attorney, where we went over all the findings. Our next big question was who holds the mortgage. Was it my name or James'? The deed had my name listed, but we would have to call to find out the details on the mortgage. While on hold, we all prayed. The clerk on the phone asked for my social security number, as it was needed to access the account. After I provided it, she replied with, "Hmm, that's strange. You are not listed on this mortgage, so I cannot release any information to you at this time." I screamed with excitement, a huge weight lifted off my shoulders. After filing paperwork for Dissolution of Marriage, I headed home.

As I walk into the house, I was greeted with walls of boxes. Nearly my entire house was packed. I followed the voices in the house to my bedroom where there was nothing left. Nothing. It was all gone. I remember collapsing back into the wall and sliding down to the floor, completely overcome with grief. Heartbroken. Once we were so excited to move into this house. Our first home, that we had purchased, as a couple. Now, I would be leaving with our children. It all seemed to be happening so fast. It felt like I was just standing still and everything around me was crumbling. I wish I could say that it was so easy to call on the Lord in those days, but I couldn't even form a prayer. I leaned on the prayers being lifted up on my behalf.

I spent most of the time just asking people what I should do. "Just tell me what to do," I'd say, because I couldn't comprehend making a decision, let alone one that might be wrong. In the end, all I could do was trust in the Lord. I knew He was present. I knew He gave leadership and direction. I knew He had great compassion for us and that His heart was broken and grieved by the circumstances surrounding us. That was my solace, my comfort.

Later that evening, as we all sat around the table trying to have a meal together, my phone kept receiving text messages from James and Jessica. They had already found out that I had gone to the Sheriffs' Department. Both were blaming and accusing me of being vengeful. Neither of them could even begin to see that it was their actions that had brought this upon all of us. It was as if they were blind.

Time seemed to almost stand still, like a drip hanging on the end of a faucet, refusing to let go. When Thursday did finally arrive, I took the boys to their school bus with cupcakes for their classes. I cried as I tried to explain to their bus driver that this would be their last day at school. The boys had such wonderful teachers. They were so thoughtful of the boys during these last few days. They had given the boys each a school shirt signed by every member of their class. They would also send cards to them in the mail. Not to be outdone, their

Sunday school class would also send cards handmade by those in Children's Church. The boys still have every card, as well as the t-shirts. My favorite card was written by a six year-old little girl. Addressed to Josiah, it read, "I will miss your brother, but I don't miss you yet." Hilarious.

After my last appointment with the attorney, as I paid her the filing fee for the divorce, I was struck by how God had worked in extraordinary ways to provide for each need throughout the whole process. One way that He blessed me was with an attorney who deeply cared for me. She withheld all her fees and only charged the filing fee. Second, the Lord would use our church to bless me with love offerings that met all the necessary fees and unplanned costs. I would later participate in Divorce Recovery[v] and learn just how unbelievable it is to have an attorney care more about you than your bill.

When the boys arrived home from school, a few beloved friends were there to say goodbye to us. Leaving brought such a wave of emotion. This was the home James and I had made together. The first home we ever purchased. In that house stood friends I had to leave, members of a church that had been so overwhelmingly good to me. It was as if a death occurred, and we were leaving someone behind. I guess, in reality, it was a death. We would never be *that* family anymore. We would never be the same again.

Pulling out of the driveway, my dad drove the U-Haul, some others drove his truck filled with other items, the boys and I in our van, while my mom and sister followed in her SUV. It snowed that day, turning our three hour trip into six hours. We were more than exhausted when we crossed into West Virginia. As I reached out to pay the bridge toll, the attendant told me "You are taken care of Ma'am." Poor guy didn't know what to do when he looked in to see tears running down my face.

Finally, at my parents' home, all I could think to do was crawl into bed. Both boys slept in bed with me that night and would continue to do so for the next two weeks.

Chapter Twelve

A week or so later, on January 16, the divorce would be reported in our town newspaper, leaving so many confused. Several expressed their disappointment in me; they felt like I hadn't even tried, but I never could, nor would, come to the place where I could tell them everything. There was just too much.

Sue Birdseye, in her book, *When Happily Ever After Shatters*, shared that she learned from her attorney and counselor that adulterers often don't make the final move to end their marriage. "Sadly, it was usually the betrayed spouse who was forced to make the difficult decision."[vi] This was true in our case. When I found out about the affair, James had already moved on. He no longer saw us as a married couple; but rather as a means to an end.

At my parents' home, life went on. About a month into living there, I would find a place to work. Actually, it kind of found me. God opened the doors for me to care for a handicap girl whose parents attended the church I was now a part of. They were gracious to help me and very understanding about giving me time off when I needed it. That was just the first of many blessings the

Lord would provide as I struggled with finding my new normal.

Shortly after settling in a little more, I went to my first Divorce Recovery. Looking back on it now, I cannot imagine my journey without this group. They were a huge help to my own mental health and healing. Although that first night was quite an "inner battle" for me, I ended up attending for about two years. Yet, that first night, I kept thinking, "I don't belong here. James and I were the ones to help people when their marriages needed this kind of support." What a humbling experience to come to know *their* genuine support and love. They, too, were going through, or had gone through, what I was trying to navigate. They helped me begin the process of understanding that this event in my life did *not* define me. They became my cheerleaders when I felt so defeated and discouraged.

I remember one night sharing about how difficult things had been. In response, for two weeks, they came and brought food for the boys and me. Gift cards would be slipped into my hands, toys for the boys, and groceries left sitting on our porch. Things, needs I had prayed specifically for, God was providing through His people.

74

Looking back, I can see my Heavenly Father's fingerprints all over their ministry to us. He hadn't left us nor abandoned us.

One Wednesday morning on the way to work, I received a call from Detective Carl Smith. He quickly informed me the Grand Jury was meeting, and he would call me as soon as they made a decision as to whether or not bring charges against James. About two o'clock that afternoon, he called back with difficult news. Jessica had, we allege, committed perjury and the prosecutor did not have enough evidence without her testimony. In the State of Ohio, without the victim's testimony, no charges could be filed. Even with the journal, and all its explicit details, he would go without being charged. I left early from work that day because my emotions were lost to me. Our lives had taken such a devastating blow, and yet there was nothing that could be done. I came into Divorce Recovery that night in need of deep support. Those wonderful people shared in my struggle to put it all in place.

That evening, I would leave the group setting to meet with the pastor of the church where our group met, Kurt Busiek. He kindly listened and offered his full support.

After I shared with him what the boys and I had been through, he offered me the priceless gift of professional Christian counseling; at no cost to me. I will forever be in debt to him and the church for that gift. Four years later, my boys and I still see that same counselor Dr. James Patrick Ward. God has used Dr. Ward to help walk me through the stages of grief. And when I wanted to linger on one step, he had patience and allowed me to process before I moved on.

Yet, he also pushed me forward when necessary. Someone once said the road to recovery was not a couch. Jesus told the lame man to get up and walk! I learned to allow myself time to deal with my anger; but to practice caution and not allow myself to linger there. It was too tempting, and I refused to allow the devil a foothold.

Truly, Dr. Ward has not only been there for me, but he has been there for the boys as a mentor and listening ear.

Chapter Thirteen

James once said, "They (the boys) will hate you one day." He was right.

That hate packed a powerful punch in Samuel's life particularly. As the oldest, it hit him hardest, and he held so much anger towards me during those first few months. He simply couldn't understand why I didn't tell him details of what happened. Sam, like me, had to walk through those same steps of grief, and it took nearly four years. But, the entire time, God was at work in the heart of my oldest.

2 Chronicles 20:15,17 reads, "This is what the Lord says to you: 'Do not be afraid or discouraged because of this vast army. *For the battle is not yours, but God's.* You will not have to fight this battle. Take up your positions; *stand firm* and see the deliverance the Lord will give you. Do not be afraid do not be discouraged. Go out to face them tomorrow and the Lord will be with you"[vii] (emphasis mine).

March 11, 2011 was the Divorce Court date. My mom would travel with me to Brown County (Georgetown, Ohio) as a support. As we sat in the hallway of the courthouse waiting for Nikki to arrive, James walked in.

I don't remember if we even spoke to one another. I just remember a lot of emotion and awkwardness. Unbelievably, the whole process would come to an end in just a few minutes, yet it was all so raw and fresh in my mind and heart. Nikki gave me some great advice that day that I will never forget. "Don't allow him to see you cry."

Divorce strips you of who you once were; a wife, a lover, a best friend, and so on. I would have to find out who I was without him. Inside the courtroom, the attorneys and judge went over what we had decided on our own and then asked me two questions. The first, "Are you pregnant?" Quick answer, "No." The second, "Do you want to change your name back to your maiden name?" Again, quick answer, "No." Gavel bangs, dissolving ten and a half years of marriage in less than thirty minutes. I've waited longer for a pizza!

I spent months planning our wedding. Dress, shoes, meal, guests, et cetera. It all seemed so foolish now. But I had loved him. In spite of the regretful way my marriage ended, I still gained two amazing boys that have brought so much joy and pride into my life. Years of ministry that God allowed us to share will always be such a reward for me. After James and his attorney walked out of the courtroom that day, I cried. It was all I could do to hold it in until they left.

It was finally over.

In her book, *When He Leaves*, Kari West shares a helpful exercise concerning marriage. Calling the exercise "Fact or Fiction,"[viii] she encouraged setting up dual lists, labeling one "Fact" and the other "Fiction." Under "Facts about My Marriage" I wrote, *ten and a half years were good. I enjoyed working in ministry with James. I allowed him to define me and my abilities.* Under "Fiction about My Marriage" I wrote, *all ten and a half years were bad. Going into ministry was a big mistake. I could have done more to save my marriage. My life is ruined by the divorce.*

Moving onto my children, I created "Facts about My Children." *I am doing the best I can for my boys. Even though I have primary custody, they will see inconsistencies between lifestyles. Our relationship is different now. They both belong to God.* "Fiction about My Children:" *I am the only one who can help my boys. It's all their dad's fault. Changes that I make to please them will help our relationship. I could have done more to make things better for them.*

Whenever I look over these lists, it helps me keep perspective. After all, reality is always shaped by our perception of it.

Those next few days would be so hard. As I struggled in newfound single motherhood, James seemed to be thriving in his new relationship with Jessica. For me the divorce felt like a giant wall, for him it seemed like a ramp he used to jumpstart a whole new life! There were Facebook posts like, *Having a date with a beautiful woman...*written on the day of our divorce!

After a year or so in counseling, Dr. Ward suggested a woman's Bible study that would be great for me, since I needed to make friends. Even though I was living again in my hometown, most of my friends from high school had moved away. Therefore, this new group would be a place where I could be introduced to new friends and share in the Scriptures as well. Soon I found a Bible Study that met on Thursday mornings. The women had already begun digging into the book of Genesis and were half-way through. I won't ever forget my first lesson. Vanessa Tunnel, the leader, began with the question,

"How many of you really know what it is like to be asked of God to leave your home, family, friends, and your job to move to a place He would choose?" Ahem, ding-ding, we have a winner right here in Aisle Five!

In God's call to Abraham, He said, "Go from your country your people and your father's household to the land I will show you. I will make you into a great nation and I will bless you; I will make your name great and you will be a blessing. And I will bless those who bless you, and whoever curses you I will curse; and all the people on earth will be blessed through you."[ix] In bringing up this Scripture passage from Genesis 12, was Vanessa speaking directly to me? How could she have known this was my story as well? It was yet another confirmation that this was where God wanted me in this season in life.

Do you remember when you were in grade school and you wanted to ask someone to be your friend? If so, you may have passed them a piece of paper that read, "Yes, No, Maybe." Well, that was how I felt at my first discussion group with these ladies. At the end of my first study with them, they were taking prayer requests. I blurted out amongst the group that I desperately needed friends in this season I was walking through-- it seemed to come out like "word vomit." It was *all* out before I could take it back!

At first, it was the sound of proverbial crickets rubbing their legs together in a far corner of the room. Then, one lady started scribbling on paper, tore it from her notebook, and passed it to me. It was her cell number, with a note that said, "Text me!" Suddenly, I had flashbacks from gym class when the "cool kid" picked you to be on their team for dodge ball. She picked me! From there, Emily Vernon and I became the best of friends. Before long, many of the ladies in the group reached out to me as well.

More gifts from the Lord.

Chapter Fourteen

On March 28, 2012, I woke up feeling well. However, by mid-morning, I began to experience a migraine coming on. Later that day, I ended up in urgent care where they would give me the traditional migraine cocktail. It did little to nothing. I was back in a few days. This time, they ordered some tests and gave me an IV infusion with some stronger medications. I went for an MRI on a Friday night, and they called with the results on Monday. I was instructed to see a neurologist because it appeared as though I had a tumor on the base of my brain. Umm, what did you just say?

Thankfully, doctors quickly discovered that I had a small Arachnoid cyst and not a tumor. It was not pressing on anything and not inhibiting the flow of any fluids; so they would just monitor it and watch for any changes. I was then referred to another neurologist who began with acupuncture, trigger point injections, nerve blocks and Botox. All of these treatments got me by for a few days, but then the pain would come back in full force. The Botox treatment I received was very aggressive and led to six weeks of physical therapy to regain range of motion in my neck. It didn't take long before my finances were exhausted, yet we seemed to be no closer to an answer.

Still another neurologist stepped in and referred me to West Virginia University, but I would not be able to secure an appointment for over six months. The waiting was so difficult. A few months prior, I had to make the hard decision to file for disability. I had been living off our savings for six months, paying all our bills as well as several emergencies along the way. But, as God showed Himself true once again, generous friends stepped in and provided. They sold a car of theirs and felt led by the Lord to send me a check from the sale. Meanwhile, I was eventually granted disability…with only $200 left in our savings. Again, the Lord's timing was perfect.

Now, on a fixed income, we continued to trust God to provide. I was accepted into the West Virginia University Cares program by a neurologist who did everything he could to help my case move forward. After our first initial appointment with Dr. David Watson, it was clear he was going to do all he could to help me find the cause to my pain. Quickly, he was able to diagnose and confirm that I had Dystonia, Occipital Neuralgia, and Chronic Migraine. With some changes in my medicine regimen, we began what he felt was the best treatment plan. I would continue to see him for a year and a half. Over that time, I would be given nerve blocks monthly. Then, on April 15 2012, I had a procedure called Cryo-ablation for the nerve pain. Effectually, it was a procedure designed to freeze the nerve they believed to be causing the problem. If it was successful, my pain could be significantly reduced.

The surgery itself was a nightmare. The twilight sedation did little to nothing to keep me under. I woke up midway through the procedure and tried to sit up. A nurse was forced to hold my head down until it was finished. The pain was near unbearable. And, after all that, the surgery did not even work. In fact, it seemed to *increase* my pain!

From there, we felt the next step was to try something called an Occipital Nerve Stimulator. At that point, I was willing to try anything, even though it promised to be a long process beginning at the Pain Clinic. To qualify, I would have to fail *three* nerve blocks. I clearly remember Dr. Watson getting on his phone while we were still in the room, trying to get me into the pain psychologist that day. He succeeded and literally ran with us to show us right where we needed to go. I'm grateful for his determination. I had not ever had a doctor fight so hard to get me help.

Sadly, all the planning and preparation for this surgery also failed. My insurance denied it. They tried every way they knew possible. They even had doctors who were willing to donate their time. But insurance would not cover the device itself which was well over $150,000.

The road of pain is isolating. It can consume you when you're are unable to do the things you used to or want to. It led me down a road of depression and discouragement. Three times insurance would deny my surgery, and it felt like we had hit a wall. Finally, the doctors at West Virginia University hospital and Pain Clinic were unable to do any more for me. That was a difficult pill to swallow. I was beginning to lose all sense of hope. Surely, God could see my need. Surely, He cared that I was desperate. Could this really be His will for my life?

By 2013, James and Jessica would be expecting their first child—a little girl. Sitting the boys down on the couch one night, it felt like déjà vu. It was hard for them to process that they would soon have a new half-sister and a step-mom to adjust to. Even though some time had passed, the boys had not seen Jessica since we left the church and didn't even know she was the "other woman."

I feel so blessed for the cherished people God placed in our lives to stand alongside of us and lift us up in prayer during that time. Those were some very trying days for the boys and me, and we could not have gotten through them without their prayers and support. The boys, in particular, were struggling. Their dad had changed so much. He had left, and they were unsure of who he really was anymore.

Each day, the boys and I learned how to better handle our new normal. Each of us grew stronger and more confident that things were in fact going to be okay. They would be attending a private school through a generous gift from my parents. They would see their dad once a month. And, over the summer, they would get about three weeks of visitation time. It was a hard adjustment for all of us, but I love how God taught each of us patience and courage in the midst of chaos.

Chapter Fifteen

One day, I simply needed to get out of the house, so I took a trip to the mall. I ran into a lady from church, Lisa Copenhaver, and we started talking. Sharing with her how alone I felt on this journey, she asked if I would be interested in doing a book study with her--just the two of us. I think she even surprised herself; it hadn't been anything she had been planning. I said, "Yes," before she had a chance to change her mind!

"I don't know what made me say that," she answered back. But God knew I would need her.

After some prayer, we decided on Tim Keller's book, *Walking with God through Pain and Suffering.* I had just purchased the book, so I was excited to study it with someone. Neither one of us had any idea how God would anoint that time together. I had never been a part of a book study so unique. Lisa would prepare questions a few days before our study, then we would go over them when we met together. Our "book study" led to times of deep intercession and fasting. I would explain to Lisa that the whole journey through pain felt much like I was caught in the middle of a stormy sea, waves tossing me about. There was a ship ahead of me with all of my loved ones, including my boys, but no matter how hard I tried I could not get to them. It was all I could do to keep my nose above the water. I felt as if I was wearing those silly kid "floaties" on my arms, but they were leaking air. It was a desperate time.

As a migraine sufferer, I can tell you the frustration my fellow sufferers and I feel because the pain isn't visible. We don't wear casts or bandages, nor do we walk with a limp. By all accounts, we appear "normal." But our pain isolates us, cripples us, and changes how we see ourselves. Many will treat us as though it is all made up in our heads. Well, truthfully the pain is in our heads! Yet, it is very *real* and very *debilitating.* Indeed, it is a misunderstood pain at best.

While I was in that book study with Lisa, I felt like I hit a wall with my treatment at West Virginia University. Without approval for the surgery, the doctors didn't feel like there was much more they could do for me except nerve blocks once a month. The discouragement and depression hit me hard. I truly fell like the psalmist in Psalm 13. "How long, O Lord? Will you forget me forever? How long will you hide your face from me? How long shall I take counsel in my soul, having sorrow in my heart daily! How long will my enemy be exalted over me?" [x]

Thankfully, that is not the end of the Psalm. Despite the pain and confusion, still there was trust. "But I trusted in your mercy; my heart shall rejoice in your salvation. I will sing to the Lord because he has dealt bountifully with me."[xi]

Soon after Lisa and I completed our first book together, we began another...and another...and then another. Five book studies later, we are still continuing on this path together. Each time, God allowed us to add precious women to this unique circle. We have laughed, cried, prayed, and held one another through tremendous opposition from the enemy. It seemed like the closer we grew to one another, the more we experienced spiritual warfare.

However, in the midst of all of this, it appeared like I was losing ground. There seemed no relief in sight for my pain. Lisa, being the most compassionate person you will ever meet, took it upon herself to put a call into Cleveland Clinic. Looking back now, I find it quite humorous. The poor Cleveland Clinic didn't stand a chance. Lisa had been in prayer, and she would not settle for "No" from the receptionist. By the end of their conversation, I had an appointment, and one special nurse there praying for God's best for me.

My appointment was the following week. At first, the idea of "starting fresh" with a new doctor was not appealing at all. I had been down this road many times. But, at my first appointment, it was made clear that they would do all they could to get me answers at a rate that surprised us all. God was making all things new in His time. I wish I could say I didn't waver or doubt His timing, but that would be a lie. It would be such a hard lesson to learn especially when you feel like you are at the end of your rope. However, I would learn that when you are at the end of your rope; that is when you tie a knot and hang on tight.

My first appointment would be with a neurologist who felt very confident that with some medication changes, I would be on the road to recovery. I was able to get in with neurosurgeon Dr. Sean Nagel within the next two weeks. The timeline felt unbelievable. However, I shouldn't have been surprised. We had prayed and asked God for His favor, and He was at work. Nevertheless, as

I waited over that two-week stretch, my hopefulness seemed to dim as my pain increased.

One particular day, as we met in this ladies' Bible study, four wonderful women surrounded me and interceded on my behalf. They literally carried me to Jesus just like cripple's the four friends did in Mark 2:1-12. My four were desperate, and they carried me to the proverbial roof top and pulled apart the roof piece by piece until they could lower me down before Jesus. And God heard their prayers that day. After meeting with the neurosurgeon, I would get a call for a surgery date in December, 2012. They had been able to gain approval for the Occipital Nerve Stimulator on the first try. However, after I completed the routine pre-op blood work, it was found that I had a rather high white blood cell count. Therefore, they could not operate. God knew best, and my surgery was rescheduled for January, 2013.

This first surgery would be for temporary placement of the stimulator. The device itself would be outside of my body and only the leads would be implanted. This trial would last one week. After that week, if I felt at least fifty percent pain relief, I could move forward with permanent placement. I would have to remain in

Cleveland that week for follow up appointments. This meant I would need to have someone stay with me to drive me back and forth to the Clinic. That is when my pastor and his wife stepped in. Chris, my pastor's wife, stayed with me throughout the week and her husband, Glenn, would come and take me for surgery.

The day before surgery, I had six pre-op appointments. It was so much to take in, and Chris was there with me through it all. She, too, is a fellow "migrainer" and suffers a great deal with debilitating pain. We often feel like we speak a unique language with one another rarely using words because we understand the pain the other one feels. That evening she became very sick with a migraine of her own. She would call Glenn to come. He arrived an hour before I needed to be at the hospital for surgery. Not once did Glenn or Chris make me feel or treat as though I was a burden. I knew they deeply loved and cared for me, and they were committed for the long haul.

After surgery, I lay in recovery totally discouraged. I only felt burning each time they turned on the device and that was not supposed to be happening! Thankfully, the tech asked if we could wait an hour and try it all over again. I'm thankful for that because, after everything settled down, I was able to try the device again without the burning sensation. I would return a few days later to have it adjusted. As each day passed, the pain became less and less. When the trial period was over, I felt like I had at least fifty percent less pain.

In the office that Friday, doctors would remove the leads and the stitches. I was free to return home in preparation for the permanent procedure in February. During the permanent procedure, however, there were problems with the leads burning. The surgeon was confident he could successfully place one lead, but I asked if he could try for two. Thankfully, he was able to place two leads and have all the wires connected and functioning. The surgery itself lasted three hours. Time spent in recovery would be used to learn all the procedures necessary to adjust the settings and recharge the battery.

I now have another incision on the back of my head where the leads begin. They travel across the back of my head horizontally, while the wires that connect them to the battery pack run down my neck just under the skin. The battery pack, aka the "brain," rests on my collarbone. A two-inch scar is there to remind of its presence. Everyone who knew me before this surgery commented that my countenance had changed. I appeared hopeful and seemingly in less pain. It was true. I felt like I had been given a fresh new start--with a lot less pain. I would have to return about eight more times to the Clinic to have my device readjusted as I became more comfortable with how it worked.

To accept God's plan may not have come "packaged" like I planned. Nevertheless, in the process, I learned so much about myself and even more about Him. I learned that it was okay to lean into the support of treasured friends. It doesn't mean you are a failure or a burden if you need to rely on others. There will be a season in their life when you can take on the role of support and helper. In this way, everyone gets blessed.

Chapter Sixteen

Single parenting at its finest.

God has empowered and equipped me with everything I need to succeed in single parenting. James 1:5-6 reminds me that, "If any of you lacks wisdom, he should ask God, who gives generously to all without finding fault, and it will be given to him. But when he asks he must believe and not doubt, because he who doubts is like a wave of the sea, blown and tossed by the wind." Not all callings are easy, and parenting is far from that! I cannot be *everything* for my boys. They have, and will continue to learn, they are able to do far more themselves than they ever could with my help. I want them to know responsibility and hard work. I have taught them, using the help of many men along the way, how to be honorable and respectful.

Single-parenting is hands down one of the hardest jobs in the world. I didn't think I could be this tired and live to tell the story! It's exhausting. Especially when there are more of them than there are of you. I am a referee, child psychologist, cheerleader, taxi, guidance counselor, chef, personal shopper, accountant/or Bank of Mom, and, last but not least, the one who gets to say the Last

Word. All of this can be so incredibly lonely at times, leaving one longing for someone to help shoulder the responsibilities of running a house. Someone to help make the big decisions or contribute financially.

We take nothing for granted. Sure, we love popcorn and a movie at the theater, but the reality is I cannot afford that as often as we would like. So let's do popcorn and a movie at home. When the boys ask to go camping, we set up the tent in the back yard and roast S'mores over the fire. You can still have fun on a budget!

That first year we were on our own, we would not have made it without the help of my parents and many friends. With no child support the first eleven months after the divorce, I needed to have a budget that worked for us as well as helped us save at the same time. I did all I could to put money into a savings account. We only carried the debt of my student loan at the time, so we were learning to live within our means. There was nothing glamorous about the lifestyle, but I wouldn't trade a day for all the money in the world. It was always amazing to see how God provided when we prayed together. And, if there was a need, I was honest about it--like when we needed to sell our van and find a small car that was easy on gas. God always provided. In that instance, He sent a young girl our way who was paying her way to the mission field. What better way to buy a car? I got a good-mileage vehicle, while she got money for her mission trip!

When I had to have surgery about six months after we arrived in West Virginia, the doctor, who was my Ob/Gyn when I had Josiah, performed it. The bill was six thousand dollars, and I had no insurance! I waited two weeks before calling to make payment arrangements. As I explained to the receptionist what I could afford to pay each month (which wasn't much), there was a pause on the other end of the line.

"Hmm," the receptionist started. "That's weird. Your balance is paid in full. You owe nothing."

What? How can that be? I haven't paid anything. At my next follow up, I shared this with my doctor who only grinned. He'd written everything off; including the anesthesiologists. God met our need.

Another time, one Christmas, there was a knock on the door. I didn't answer because I had come home early from Bible study and already put on my PJ's! When I didn't answer the knock, the phone rang. When I didn't answer the phone, he left a message. It simply stated that there was an envelope waiting for me between the front and screen doors. Inside were ten crisp, brand new hundred dollar bills! What?!? I immediately called him back, and he said he was just the delivery guy for some friends of his. They wanted to make sure we had a great Christmas. I passed on my thanks and begged him to tell me who it was. He wouldn't budge, only adding that he would pass on my thanks. I sat down and cried.

This has happened twice. And both times, you guessed it, I cried. It still amazes me how God provides and hears our prayers. And, if I shared a request with the boys, we celebrated when God answers! All along our way, He has continually met our needs again and again. We learned to live a truth I found by author Angela Thomas, in her book, *My Single Mom Life.* In it, she writes that we must "lean into His promises with the full weight of our hope. Banking on His faithfulness."[xii]

One of the hardest things about being a divorced parent is when the boys have asked me questions, looking for the details and the whys. The boys were so young when we divorced, just six and eight. At that age, giving them all the reasons why was never an option. I have told them from the very beginning that I will always be honest with them, but there are some things I simply cannot talk about.

Our counselor gave me a great illustration given by Corrie ten Boom's Father. In her book, *The Hiding Place,* Corrie had asked her father a difficult question regarding an adult issue. She writes, "He turned and looked at me, as he always did when answering a question, but to my surprise he said nothing. At last he stood up, lifted his traveling case from the rack over our heads, and set it on the floor. 'Will you carry it off the train, Corrie?' He said. Corrie stood up and tried unsuccessfully to lift the case. 'It's too heavy,' she told her father. 'Yes,' he replied. 'And it would be a pretty poor Father who would ask his little girl to carry such a load. It's the same way, Corrie, with knowledge. Some knowledge is too heavy for children. When you are older and stronger you can bear it. For now you must trust me to carry it for you.'"[xiii]

As Samuel has gotten older, I have given him more thorough answers to his questions, but with no detail. I know he has to work through his own issues with the divorce. Many of the pieces he has put together on his own, causing him to ask hard questions, and taking time to process the answers when it hasn't been what he wanted to accept as true.

Indeed, divorce is a painful process...for children and adults.

I take my new role as a single mom seriously. One day I will stand before God for how I raised and influenced my boys. This, of course, doesn't mean that I haven't messed up or blown it on occasions. In those times, though, there has been forgiveness and grace from the boys, and we have learned how to better handle our circumstances. Sometimes, I've made a hard decision and said, "No" to things that others may allow, but I want to minister to their hearts and minds. I want to break the vicious cycle of their father's sins. For that reason, I am very selective as to what we watch together as a family.

We do not have cable television in our home for two reasons. First is the cost. Second, I want to closely monitor what my family watches. (This doesn't mean if you have cable TV we believe you are sinning. That couldn't be further from the truth. It is just what we need to do as a family.) I know what is on the boys' I-Pods and cell phones. Each of them have set restrictions. We have the Internet, but they cannot access it from their phones. If they need to use the Internet for homework or something else, they must use the home computer, which is set up so the screen is visible at all times.

We have talked openly about pornography, and both of them have committed to protecting their minds. However, as many a parent can testify, a commitment is not always enough. Safeguards should be set in place, and I will never apologize to them for the part I play in that. Studies have shown that roughly half of married Christian men, as well as multitudes of pastors, are secretly masturbating to porn. Further, it has been proven that a porn addiction is harder to break than cocaine addiction, and porn addicts are more likely to relapse than any other type of addict. I'm in the fight for the protection of my boys' hearts and minds. I'm grateful for the men in our church who have stepped in to mentor the boys--not just to help them learn how to handle life better but also how to grow into the man God wants them to be. That might look like a lunch date with the youth pastor, paintballing with a godly father, a

Father/Son Retreat with a mentor, or so many other instances.

For both Samuel and Josiah's thirteenth birthdays, I asked twenty-six men combined, who have been active in my boys' lives, to write them each a letter of encouragement, advice, or whatever else the Lord laid on their hearts. When we celebrated these birthdays, two years apart, I gave each all of the letters in a basket with fifty dollars. Neither could believe that those men would take the time to write letters. Samuel, in particular, after he finished reading them, told me that those letters were his greatest gift. What better way to tell him, and his brother, that we are not alone in this. God has chosen over two dozen men in one way or another to impact their lives for the greater good.

Chapter Seventeen

Eight Promises to My Children:

- I will try to be the best parent I can be.

- I will make time during the week just for you.

- I will take good care of myself, so I can better care for you.

- I will allow you to be my child, not expect you to be my caregiver.

- I will be available to you anytime; I'll expect the same courtesy of you.

- I will model the values of fairness, honesty, and forgiveness.

- I will not speak against your dad. I'll apologize if I do.

- I will get up one more time than I'm knocked down.

- *When I try and fail, please forgive me. I love you. [xiv]

I never dreamed I would be where I am today. I don't think anyone plans to go through a divorce. Regardless, even if my family's life now seems like a reality show, this is where we are. Our only option is to move forward, allowing the Lord to teach us as we go. If we move forward, and miss the lessons along the way, all was in vain. God may have wanted so much for me in marriage, but He still is able to move and work now that I am a single mom.

I will never forget my first visit to the doctor's after my divorce. Needing to update my paperwork, I came to the part that asked about marital status. "Divorced" seemed to stand out in all caps! More than that, the word felt tattooed on my forehead. And, let's face it, it can feel just as isolating within the body of Christ. Try selecting a small group that fits you. You're single, but you have children…and they're not necessarily little anymore. You're older (long gone are the twenties) than the *normal* singles' group, so you don't really fit there either. You can participate in a married with children group, but you are suspiciously "one man down." Suddenly, you start to feel like you did in elementary school gym class when you were picked last for every game. This doesn't mean you pick up your toys and go home, refusing to participate. It just means this is going to require more work than you planned. "There is no preparation for the possibility that one partner--even a Christian, even the one you believed God led you to-- may have a hidden agenda or character defect. God does not always keep us safe. Praying together does not guarantee staying together. Too often a divorced Christian is invisible in the church. Misplaced and without identity." [xv]

My relationship with James is obviously very different today than it was when we were married. He will always be the father of our boys, but his role has changed. I learned early on to do all I could to guard my heart when I knew I would be seeing him. Not because I held romantic feelings but because of the hurt and bitterness that I knew would be waiting for me. I must confess that we had some heated exchanges a time or two, and we both have realized that did nothing for our relationship with the boys. I had to set boundaries to safeguard that. So I do not allow him into my home, not even into the entryway. Parenting six hours away has not always worked well for him. I appreciate the fact that he has allowed me to parent and discipline the boys the way I see fit.

I would not ever wish the pain of divorce on anyone, but those who have felt its bitter sting understand. And this understanding has changed their lives forever...and not in a bad way! Kari West shares in her book, *When He Leaves*, that the power of divorce is an illusion. "It doesn't rip off your relationship with God. It wilts under the heat of passion for life. It stops short of robbing every hope. It fades in the light of good humor. It doesn't disrobe you of dignity. It cannot take your courage. It is dis-empowered by joy. It capitulates to optimism. It is disarmed by truth. Its pain is temporary. It is starved by faith. Its time is limited."[xvi] The key to unmasking the illusion of divorce, however, is forgiveness. Without a doubt, forgiveness is a crucial step in any relationship. I would say it is impossible to move forward and be emotionally healthy without taking the time to forgive the offender. That is not to say that the road to forgiveness is an easy road. In reality, the road is painful. I will never forget walking into Dr. Ward's office for the first time. Looking right at me, he asked, "Tell me what brings you here." An hour later and I still felt like I had only just begun answering that one question!

Our second session began with me announcing, "If you could just give me the five steps I need to move on, I will be out of your hair."

I think, perhaps, he laughed out loud. Four years later, I now realize that this journey is definitely much longer than just five steps. Forgiveness is hard. Don't ask me exactly how many steps are in this journey. I am far from sure. But of this I am sure, the first step must involve forgiveness. No one moves forward until an unforgiving spirit is dealt with. Unfortunately, dealing with such a spirit is much like a root canal. Above the gum line, your tooth may look great. Underneath, however, there is "infection," and it must be removed. Yes, it's painful. Excruciating even. But if you don't do the work to remove the root, you will never be well. You will be stuck and being "stuck" can be really ugly at times.

The times I struggled with holding onto an unforgiving spirit were so deceiving. I felt I had this illusion of control. I had no control. I wasn't hurting him by holding onto any of it; I was only hurting myself. Catherine Claire Larson writes in her book, *As We Forgive,* "Forgiveness does not mean that what happened didn't matter. It isn't sweeping a crime under the rug. It isn't saying the crime was a misunderstanding. It isn't saying that the crime did little harm or that it left no loss in its wake. Forgiveness isn't forgetting. Forgiveness isn't usually a one-time act, but more commonly a lifetime commitment. Finally, and most important, forgiveness is excruciatingly difficult."[xvii]

I learned all too quickly that I could not forgive on my own. I am only able to forgive as I accept the Lord's forgiveness for my own sins. There was no place for me to take a self-righteous role. I was not blameless. I could not say I was without sin. No, I did not choose to commit the sin of adultery, but I was (and still am) in need of a Savior's forgiveness. Forgiveness is about relinquishing control, or the idea of control, that you will be justified. It's about letting go and allowing God to have His way in the matter. It is unlikely He will rain big balls of fire down from Heaven on those who wronged us or inflict boils all over the butts of those we can't stand, so we have to let it go!

Forgiveness doesn't fit into my box as neat and pretty as I would like it too. It took me two full years to believe myself when I said, "James, I forgive you." I remember that day, and even more clearly, I remember how almost immediately those words would push me to lean into God's understanding and grace. It is unlikely I will ever forget what happened in December, 2010 when my life first turned upside down, and I realized I no longer recognized the man I married. Though the details are not as vivid as they once were, I can still recall every detail, every hurt, and every word.

I don't believe James will ever know, or even come close to realizing, how his decision impacted our family that day. But it is my desire that my boys will never forget the *big* and small decisions we made together to get where we are today. These hard decisions to forgive and move forward allowed God to use our story to help other families experience hope in their painful journey. I love what Pete Wilson shares in his book, *Plan B*. "He [God] knows what you're going through. He is right beside you, sharing your pain, even though He may not take it away. And He knows what He is doing with your life, even if you don't. But in order for that to make a difference in your life, you might have to change your thinking. You might have to give up some of your expectations about what God owes you and how things are supposed to be." [xviii]

So why didn't He take it all away? I mean, doesn't God want marriages to survive? What can I possibly learn from my marriage failing? I don't know the answers to those questions, but I do know this. God is still God, and

He never left us. He is walking each painful step with me and makes His presence known in so many ways. It's easy to sometimes feel "entitled" to answers and to complain that I have lost all control. But, in reality, I never had control in the first place.

Chapter Eighteen

Community is a gift.

Don't allow your pain, as deep as it may be, to keep you from fully embracing the gift of community. Don't let your disappointment, as devastating as it may be, keep you from "me too." I will never forget my first Divorce Recovery Christmas party. We gathered for food, fellowship and a white elephant gift exchange. In case you are unsure of this kind of gift exchange, it involves everyone bringing a gift under a certain dollar value. The guests each draw a number and select a gift in the order of their number from one upwards. After you have chosen your gift, the person with the number immediately following yours can "steal" your gift or choose a gift of their own.

I believe there were six women and Paul--the only guy in the group for quite a while. He had the first pick, so he selected the initial gift. He chose my gift, except that he didn't know it was mine. He had a puzzled look as he unwrapped the decorative wooden nutcracker. I quickly explained that every divorced wife deserved her own nutcracker! That little gag gift soon became the most coveted present at the party. What a great night!

Indeed, except for the members of that group, no one truly understood what I was experiencing. Whether it was trying to work a budget with no child support, managing my emotions, or the emotions of my boys, this group had "been there done that." With most of the group composed of those caught on "the other side" of adultery, they could help and support me like no other. Those amazing people showed me that if I could just laugh at the absurdity in my situation, then I could maintain some sanity. I mean, come on, my spouse chose someone who still rode a school bus!

Moreover, this community understood the pain and discouragement I felt during the holidays, because they felt it too. That initial Christmas after the divorce would become the first among many sad reminders. The boys were six hours away with their dad, and I was struck with the realization that this was my first Christmas divorced. More would follow—first birthday divorced, first anniversary divorced, et cetera. You quickly learn that you and your children must make new traditions. Still adjusting to a new normal, you start to find that you cannot stop living just because you are no longer married. You are still *you,* and your children are still very much a part of your life--so learn to *live* again, and live well.

Sure, this new life may include a new language, a divorce lingo if you will. Learn it well and grow through it. Become an expert in talking about visitation schedules, no fault divorce, mediations, primary or shared custody plans, and alimony. Be the authority on how to review and revise your decree of the court, depositions, and deciding whether or not you need a guardian-ad-litem for your children. Specialize in learning the names of judges who have sat over the cases of your friends. Be adept at discussing the process at length until you, yourself, feel like Dr. Phil.

Oh, indeed, it is all exhausting. But I thank the Lord that I was never alone. Words fail to adequately describe how pivotal my Divorce Recovery was to me and my journey. Even though we were linked by painful, yet shared, events in each other's lives, I always felt their constant love and support at every turn. If you are just at the beginning of this journey, I encourage you to seek out such a group. For me, I attended one away from my home church, because I needed the distance from what was once familiar. Everyone going through divorce needs a group that is completely confidential and safe. A place where you can unpack your baggage and experience healing and support from others in the same fight. I will never regret the hours spent in Divorce Recovery. I am a better mother and divorcee' because of their influence in my life.

Are you fully known by other believers? Are you transparent with one another? Can they speak truth into your life, even if it is painful to hear at times? It has been said that you can only be loved to the extent you are known. I experienced this firsthand in a Ladies' Bible Study group. Sharing with these women didn't mean, "Here is my rant about my ex-husband…" No, it meant coming to a place where I could admit I made mistakes too and that my faith was not where it should have been in my marriage. It meant raw honesty shared amongst beloved sisters in Christ.

I distinctly remember one time when these ladies surrounded me and told me the strengths they saw in me. I was forced to make a choice—would I believe them or not? This group of community, these special sisters of mine, helped me find my "role" again. I wouldn't be defined by the choices of my spouse any longer. As it says in Galatians 5:1, "It is for freedom that Christ has set us free. Stand firm, then, and do not let yourselves be burdened again by a yoke of slavery."[xix] I would no longer accept that I was called *"incapable."*

It was not part of my plan to be a single mom. But God knew, and He empowered me to raise the boys in a way pleasing to Him. True, I would have to step up to the plate, but He, and a special group of people, were with me each step of the way. Together, they strengthened me to learn what it meant to run a household on a strict budget, to organize chores, to teach the boys responsibility, to help them understand what roles they would play in our new normal, and so much more. Indeed, through the Lord and those ladies, I would also learn what it meant to be *hopeful* again.

Learning to believe and *hope* again is *life-giving*. I began to realize how very insulting it is to God to be a person who expects the worst. In my mind, I was limiting the power God had over situations concerning the boys. How absurd for me to think I could love them more than he did! I had to learn to *hope*, not in what I could see, but in what I could not see. I had to retrain my brain so it would come to a place of hope again. I could no longer place my hope in earthly things. I had to consciously pick up my hopes, my dreams, and my family, and place them in the hands of an Almighty God, even though this mean coming to grips with the fact that His timing is very different than mine.

As it says in Isaiah 55:9, "As the heavens are higher than the earth, so are my ways higher than your ways and my thoughts than your thoughts."[xx] Further, I had to learn to accept that I, and others, are imperfect. For as long as I can remember, I have been a perfectionist—one who often found herself disappointed in others when they failed to meet the expectations I set. True, my expectations were often unrealistic, but I would be so frustrated nonetheless. Yet, no matter how frustrated I might get with others, my greatest frustrations were reserved for me. Not wanting family and friends to view me as I viewed myself, I worked to hide all my imperfections and strove to at least *look* perfect.

After my divorce, however, there no longer was an arrogance about how I functioned around others. I began to see that my brokenness was a far greater bridge to others than my pretended wholeness had ever been. In my ladies' group, I learned that it was okay to "not have it all together." It was okay to be flawed, to be imperfect, even damaged. That is where God could begin His work in me. It was complete surrender and utter humility, but I found no other safe place like it. Through vulnerability and humiliation, I learned to leave behind what was once so familiar to me. I learned to make a choice to bravely walk in His plan for me. I learned that, despite my failings, the Lord saw me as *beautiful*.

When James' journal was turned over to the detectives, intimate details became permanent, and public, record. I felt dirty and discarded. I would be sent for testing to determine if I had any sexually transmitted diseases, even though I had never been with another. The whole process made me feel cheap and tawdry. Thankfully, the Lord, and those He placed in my life, showed me that my beauty had nothing to do with the physical. Beauty would not be found in my hair, my clothes, or even the number on the scale. It was something so much deeper. The perfectionist that I am, however, made accepting that He saw me as lovely a slow process. It took silencing the negativity that I often allowed to speak to me. It took believing that, in Him, I was enough. That deep understanding that I am loved unconditionally, even when I am at my worst, gradually sunk into the core of my being. The blessed assurance that, no matter what I did, He would still love me brought life and joy to my heart once again.

Brennan Manning beautifully once shared, "I am now utterly convinced that on Judgment Day, the Lord Jesus is going to ask each of us one question, and only one question: 'Did you believe that I love you? That I desire you? That I waited for you day after day? That I long to hear the sound of your voice?...I know your whole life story. I know every skeleton in your closet. I know every moment of sin, shame, dishonesty, and degraded love that has darkened your past. Right now I know your shallow faith, your feeble prayer life, and your inconsistent discipleship. And *My* word is this: I dare you to trust that I love you just as you are and not as you should be.'" [xxi]

If you are a single parent, or at least know one, then you understand that it is not for the faint of heart. It is the hardest job times two. I have never cried more, or questioned my own abilities more, than when I became a single mom. I quickly recognized that I could not be a Dad to my boys. I could only be their mom. Yet, where

I am weak, He is strong. He knows my need where I will fall short, and He meets that need in such amazing ways.

Through it all, I've had the privilege of praying with one of my boys to accept Christ, joyfully witnessed both of their baptisms, laughed with them, and cried with them—all as a single mom. Also, as a single mom, I nervously had "The Talk" with both of them. God gave me boldness, as I explained the covenant of marriage that is His design. We openly talked about pornography and the subtle way it has crept into our society. We set up guardrails at that time and continue to reinforce them today. They knew then that I would always fight for them and will continue to do so until my last breath.

No, we didn't sign up for this life, but we have been so blessed that the Lord has seen fit to walk with us each step of the way.

Chapter Nineteen

It has now been several years since the Christmas that changed everything. In the interim between then and now, there have been moments of beauty, but also moments that were incredibly hard. At this point, most of the difficult questions have been answered. With that being said, we've still spent many hours sitting with counselors--processing. I nearly choked when Samuel, my oldest, asked if his dad had ever been with prostitutes. I hesitantly replied, "What made you wonder about that?"

He answered, "It just seems like something Daddy would do." He then went to ask if I knew the number of women Daddy was with. I believe he deserved to know the truth. But the truth would be "Yes" and "No." Nothing more.

It was like death, but we both would walk through the five stages of grief. Beginning with denial, Samuel would have to reconcile who he thought his dad was with the reality of who he had become. While, at the same time, coming to grips with the fact that it had nothing to do with him. The next stage, anger, made several appearances in varying degrees. Certainly, he had every right to be angry, even to feel betrayed. Yet, bitterness could not be allowed. Scripture tells us in Ephesians 4:26, "In your anger, do not sin; do not let the sun go down while you are still angry."[xxii] I'm not so sure we handled that latter part of the passage well, but I am thankful for God's grace and patience. There indeed was a lot of anger. And, because I am the parent that is most present in his life, much of that anger was directed at me. Those were some hard days, days that led into weeks.

The bargaining stage would bring with it all the "What if" questions. What if I had done this? What if I had done that? What if we could go back in time and catch things sooner? What if? What if? What if? We had to realize that there was no answering those questions. It was all now part of our story. Just a thread in the tapestry that tells the story of our journey.

Stage four is depression, and depression is as deceptive as it is cruel. It plays a friend while it eats away at your soul. We knew this was a stage to get through, yet depression didn't want to part ways. Thankfully, counseling kept us talking and moving forward. Meanwhile, friends and family stayed involved to keep our heads above the water. The Lord led us to a church that would quickly become our home. Being a part of a community and learning what it truly means to lean into Him helped shoo away depression.

It took a little over two years for me, and a little while longer for Samuel, to move into the final stage-- acceptance. Everything happened so quickly with filing for divorce, moving, finding a new home, new job, et cetera, that I needed time for it all to sink in. Finally, reaching this stage was wonderful, but I soon realized that walking through the stages was not simply a one and done deal. It is a daily commitment.

The first time I publicly shared our testimony was via a four-minute video at church during Advent. The boys and I were given "Wonderful Counselor" and asked to share a bit of our journey through the healing process. Sometime after that, I would be asked to share at a Ladies' Banquet. I felt early on God wanted me to share in more detail. Well, at least more than a four-minute video would allow. There was still much that I could never share publicly.

After a lot of prayer, I wrote exactly what I believe God gave me to share. But, two weeks before my talk, our church was rocked with a scandal. I remember sitting the boys down, just like I had before, and telling them what was on the evening news. We were all devastated. Josiah cried. Samuel remained composed but progressively became more and more angry. He finally spoke up, "Mom, this feels like the worst case of déjà vu" and then he left the house.

I knew God had spoken to me clearly about what to share. But now, after that whole mess, I felt such confusion. Those were difficult days for all those at my church. Yet, God's timing is perfect. Just two weeks later, I would stand on a stage before a large group of women, and a few men, and share our message. I looked out over the crowd and saw my two boys looking straight back at me. I began by giving my two special young men credit. It was an honor and privilege to share our testimony, but I only wanted to do so with the Lord's prompting and permission from the boys.

The hardest part of that day was revealing that I had to go for testing, as I mentioned it earlier in the book. I knew in my mind that I would have to relate that story, but it as a hard step to make. James was the only man I was ever intimate with. Yet, at the clinic, they didn't care what you told them. They only wanted a name to call for next in line, and to know if you were paying with cash or credit card. A couple hours, and a couple hundred dollars later, I felt so humiliated. Later, on the same day as the testing, James would call to talk to the boys. Before he spoke with them, however, he would go on to tell me that he had been with nine other women who were better than me. "You," he said, "will never be good enough for me." He couldn't have been more right. I would never be enough for him. That's not God's design. We are only ever complete in Him.

So, standing in front of that crowd, I shared a passage from Psalm 45:13, "The royal daughter is all glorious within."[xxiii] God opened His word for me through this passage. We are all the Bride of Christ. We were all purchased at a high price. We are all the sons and daughters of the One True King—even if we don't always feel it. For example, I shared a story that night from our dinner table when we were playing a game. In the game, we were using one word to describe one another. When it was my turn to be described by the tiny humans I created, do you want to know what one word they used to describe me? "Pudgy." Not "mother," not "hero" nor "beautiful." No, he-who-shall-not-be-named, called me "Pudgy."

Of course, I have been called much worse, but it does stop and make you wonder, "How does God see me?" We may see ourselves as defeated, yet He calls us more than conquerors. We may see ourselves as abandoned, yet He tells us we will never be left nor forsaken. We may see ourselves as rejected by the world, yet He calls us Redeemed. We may see ourselves as broken, yet He calls us His beloved. We may see ourselves as hurt, yet He calls us healed. We may see ourselves as unworthy, yet He calls us honored, and we may see ourselves as failures, yet He knows our future and gives us hope.

This list goes on and on! We are defined by God and by God alone. I am not, nor have I ever been, defined by the mistakes or sins of another. I am truly the daughter of the One True King.

Chapter Twenty

Divorce has taught me that I deserve better. Not that I am someone special, but that I deserve someone who will love and cherish me as God designed. I know enough to realize that no one person will ever complete me. Only God can make a person feel whole. Moreover, divorce has taught me that without trust in your marriage, it will be very difficult to survive.

When I returned that night to our house, after being away at my friend's house for a few days. I was determined to fight for our marriage. I told him as much in the car ride home. But when I saw Jessica's pants on the armrest of the sofa, I knew then that he wasn't committed to saving our marriage. I could never trust him again. That was the beginning of letting go of who I was with James. I had allowed him to belittle and tear me down with words, yet, strangely, I still looked to him to restore what had been broken. He never could...and never would. But, again, that was never God's design.

Finally, divorce has taught me that the truth needs no defense. There were times when I spoke out against blatant lies or attacks on my character, but there were more times when God whispered to be still. Surely, so often we want to retaliate to clear our name and make things right. I wish I could say that every time this happened, I responded in a biblical manner, but that would be a lie. And, most often, when I didn't heed His warning, it only made the problem escalate. Oh, I have so much yet to learn my friends!

I discovered, through some trial and error, that James and I best communicate via text messages. And, while doing so, we work to keep it strictly related to the boys. We do have a court-stipulated visitation schedule that we do our best to follow. But, in our situation, it is more complicated because we currently live in two different states while our divorce was in a third! The schedule follows the public school schedule for the town we lived in while going through the divorce. Currently, however, the boys attend private school in a whole other state. The dates of the two school districts rarely match-up.

The visitation schedule also separates Christmas Eve and Christmas Day. Well, James and I live six hours away from one another. To follow the decree, we'd need to spend nearly the entire holiday traveling. All of this to say, we've had to make many compromises for the sake of the boys. We rotate holidays, except Thanksgiving which James takes and Christmas Day which I take. We divide Christmas break, with James always getting the latter half which includes New Year's Day. Once a month, the boys leave right after school on Friday and travel to visit with their dad then return Sunday evening. The summer is also divided based on vacations and camp schedules. It is never easy. No one wins in divorce. You quickly learn to cultivate a new normal and begin new traditions.

I never thought I would be able to manage a home on my own. Growing up, I always deferred to my parents. In marriage, I deferred to James. Now, I find, there is no one left to defer to. It's just me! Praise the Lord, though, for I am never alone. Believe me when I say my dad has graciously removed his share of deceased wildlife from my backyard. He bought me a shovel, thinking it would make his life a little easier. But, I'm sorry to say, it didn't. Moreover, he has helped complete a few major home renovations—such as adding another room in the basement. During these times, I truly appreciate how my father took time with Samuel to teach him the use of some tools.

As the boys get older, they also are becoming great helps. I was the happiest single mother on the block when Samuel became old enough to help with yard work. He mows the yard and trims the bushes, while Josiah helps with the flower beds and weeding. For the past two years, we have even washed the entire outside of the house by hand.

Divorce reminds me that God never intended us to parent alone. I can be the best mother God enables me to be, but I can never be a mother and a father to the boys. And, unfortunately, more often than not they get a rather hurried and incredibly tired momma. I am still trying to accept that I cannot meet every need. But something I am learning is that kids are some of the best grace givers.

Chapter Twenty-One

I am now just beginning to consider the role that dating may play in my life. How do I even begin to take these first steps?

I fully agree with Andy Stanley's advice from his *Guardrails* series. He strongly suggests that if you have been involved in a divorce, or other intimate relationship, that you need to commit to a year of "singlehood" before you enter into another relationship. During that time, allow God to renew your heart and mind.[xxiv] For me, even though several years have passed, I am only now beginning to consider pursuing a dating relationship. Frankly, it still scares me to death. I have not dated since 2000, the year I got married. Further, when James and I were dating, we were attending a conservative Bible College that did not allow physical touch of any kind between couples. Going on a date required paperwork to be filled out. Dating there was very structured. Now, however, it's a whole new ball game!

With children in the mix, I refuse to casually bring any guy into my home, and into the lives of my boys, without proper "vetting." In fact, we often joke that I'm certain my dad and eight very protective girlfriends will accompany me on my first date or at least follow behind us in their car. I am also fairly certain that a psych evaluation may be administered prior to this first date!

I believe God honors purity in every respect and that is not something I am willing to compromise on just because I have been married before. I have learned that no relationship is easy or without complications. Divorce was never in my vocabulary. And many were upset with me that mine came so fast after they learned that I was the one who filed. I will never regret that decision. Painful as it was. Had they all the information that I did, I'm certain they would have come to the same conclusion. And even if they would have chosen differently, I still believe I made the best decision for my boys and me. Although that was such a hard place to be in, I am certain it will be good again. But I am in no hurry. There is no rush to "fill the position." My boys will remain a priority with or without another person in my life.

Speaking of my boys, I am so proud of the young man Samuel is becoming. His maturity surpasses many his age simply because of what he has gone through. I am proud that he has sought out safe relationships with men who can disciple him in his walk with the Lord. He is full of passion, and I am excited to see what doors God will open for him. I believe that God will use his testimony for His glory.

As for Josiah, he was so young when everything happened. This fact has allowed him to adjust quickly to the changes, and he just keeps plugging along. He has such an incredible heart for others, and I know God has a unique ministry in store for him.

Chapter Twenty-Two

As I walk through this season of divorce, God continually opens doors for me to share my story with others who are hurting. Maybe it's from a post I have made on Facebook or something I have shared with a group of friends—it never ceases to amaze me the number of people who will reach out. Often it is because someone they love is going through something similar, and they want to know how they can help or if I have any suggestions for them. It's humbling to say the least.

I once read that, "When your greatest heartache becomes your greatest ministry, grace comes full circle."[xxv] I loved that quote so much, I bought the T-shirt! God graciously allowed this to become my reality, and I am continually awed that my greatest heartache has become a new area of ministry for me. As I have prayed each time someone has asked me for advice, I have found there are four points that stand out each time.

Point one is *listen*. Jill Buteyn writes, "Our desire to fix things can often get in the way of the silent support we can give by listening."[xxvi] Listening is an act of love that can be hard and often requires sacrifice.

One morning, I received a call from a close friend of mine. She asked if I could come over to her house. What I would come to find out was that she had just learned of her husband's unfaithfulness. Whenever I hear such tragic news, I am always taken back to the moment when I learned of James' unfaithfulness. The shock, the feeling of humiliation, the confusion and the list can go on and on. But there is that bond that forms immediately when I encounter someone who truly understands what I went through. It's like becoming a member of a club you never wanted to be a part of.

I began to pray as I drove to her house. I knew one of the most important things was to cover our time in prayer. If I was to share anything, it would come from Him. When I arrived, I began with the act of listening. It is hard for me to be still and not say something, especially when I am around people I feel comfortable with—and they are hurting. I want to help any way I can, but I am learning that listening is often the most effective thing I can offer.

For my friend, in that moment, the need to know she was being heard was what mattered. She needed my heart and my ear. She needed to get it out--like a poison or toxin trying to work its way to the surface. I know, for myself, I am sure that I must have repeated myself again and again in those first few weeks and months after I found out. I think, in my mind, I thought I might discover something that I had clearly missed before.

Mark Nepo has stated, "To listen is to continually give up softly, with a willingness to be changed by what we hear."[xxvii] My friend, that day, needed to know I was listening. There is a connection that forms when we truly listen to one another. Your brain changes through the process of telling your story. When you are truly heard and understood, both you and the listener undergo actual changes in the brain circuitry. There is a greater sense of emotional and relational connection, decreased anxiety, and a greater awareness of and compassion for others' suffering.[xxviii]

I am indebted to those who faithfully listened to me over and over. As I listened that day to my friend, the only thing I knew to do next was to pray.

Speaking of *prayer*, that is point two. If you are the listener, the best way you can honor your relationship with one to whom you are listening is to pray for wisdom. Scripture confirms our deep need to get wisdom. Proverbs 3:13 says, "Blessed is the man who finds wisdom, the man who gains understanding."[xxix] James 1:5 also states, "If any of you lacks wisdom, he should ask God, who gives generously to all without finding fault, and it will be given to him."[xxx] Meanwhile, Proverbs 4:6-7 says, "Do not forsake wisdom, and she will protect you; love her, and she will watch over you. Wisdom is supreme; therefore get wisdom. Though it cost all you have, get understanding."[xxxi]

When we pray, the very act changes the atmosphere around us. Prayer also opens the door for God to bring about healing. In those first moments of learning that the one you loved has betrayed you, it can be hard to be still. You want to know what to do and where to go. I remember often asking those closest to me, "Tell me what to do." I needed answers. My friend that day felt the need for answers as well. What I could offer, though, more than answers, was prayer. As she shared, I prayed. As she broke down and words failed her, I prayed. I prayed for her, her spouse, and her small children. I prayed for words and the wisdom to know if He wanted me to say anything at all. I prayed for guidance and direction. I prayed for comfort. I prayed for protection for her heart. Knowing that the enemy delights in strife, and is the author of confusion and chaos, I sought the

Lord in prayer. I know that there is a peace and stillness only found in Him, and prayer wraps us up in His arms.

This leads us to the third point, which is *direct*. First and foremost we must direct them to Jesus. This must be our primary goal--always working to direct people to Jesus. I would say a close second would be to direct them to Christian counseling, if necessary. I've said it before and will say it again—one of the greatest gifts given to me during that season was the gift of Christian counseling. That day, being present with my friend, I could have given her every step and process that worked for me, but what works for one may not work for another.

With that in mind, I must direct them to Jesus. No one can offer hope and healing like Him. Above all the noise, we must come to recognize His voice. We have all heard the statement that time heals all wounds. I would disagree to a point. I believe only Jesus can heal all wounds—and sometimes He does so through individuals He has called into counseling ministry.

Indeed, while Jesus must be the first Person we direct hurting friends to, there are also many benefits to Christian counseling. One is that it keeps you moving forward. Healing is a process. The process of forgiveness takes time. It is a daily commitment to forgive the hurt and pain that another has caused you and those you love. I believe that as we point them to Jesus, and to outside resources, we must remind them that their story is not over. Elisabeth Elliot once said, "Of one thing I am perfectly sure God's story never ends with ashes."[xxxii] We must point them to hope and healing.

The final point is *show up*. The gift of presence is priceless. Choose to step into their chaos and be present. And then stay present, for this step is not a brief one. Few will walk alongside you for the long haul. I believe God brings people into our lives for a season. However long the season of "showing up" and being present might be--I believe each and everyone He leads into that time will leave a lasting impression.

Showing up might be as simple as our physical presence. We don't have to offer any words or do anything special. Just by being there, we are communicating more than any words could offer. Don't get me wrong. If there is something that needs done around their home or a burden you can relieve, jump in. I remember friends who came and sat on my couch, and we did nothing but watch a movie. Another dropped off a meal and sat quietly with me while I ate. Someone else simply held me while I cried. Stories like these are endless.

Showing up is not always easy. But guess what? It is not about you. It's about how God can use you to be His hands and feet to those hurting. Showing up can be the greatest gift ever given or received. [xxxiii]

Epilogue

What I want my local church to hear and know about me. I want them to know:

1. I need you, and you need me! 1 Corinthians 12:27 states, "Now you are the body of Christ, and each one of you is a part of it."[xxxiv] I need *your* help physically, emotionally, and spiritually. I need to know I have a support system within my church. I need to know that just because I am single and divorced I still matter to you. I want to play my part in the church. In order to do so, I need to know that I am a part of the family as a whole.

2. I need men in my life. Don't get carried away! I need men who will stand alongside my boys and mentor them in everyday life. Teach them things like how to change a flat, how to change the oil in a car, et cetera.

3. I need resources. I need help with maintenance at my home. Sometimes simple repairs are not that simple when you don't have the tools or the knowhow to do it right. A free oil change? Well, that would be amazing! One church that James pastored had a cars' ministry. It was a

group of men who did car repair for people (a lot of whom were single moms) who could not afford to pay. Free babysitting is another thing. A lot of churches will do this during the holidays, which is great, but a single mom needs that help more than once a year.

4. I need a small group designed with me in mind. I no longer fit into the traditional small group, and I know I am not alone in this. We need care groups for the single and divorced people in our congregations. We are in a unique position in our lives, and we need the gift of community for such a time as this.

---

[i] For more information regarding the Emmaus Walk please see Emmaus.upperroom.org

[ii] Psalms 103:1-12 (New International Version)

[iii] Isaiah 54:4-17 (New International Version)

[iv] Giglio, Louie, Matt Gilder, Matt Redman, Chris Tomlin, and Charlie Hall. *How Great Is Our God.* 268generation, 2007. CD.

[v] Divorce Recovery Groups near you can be found online at DivorceCare.com for more details.

[vi] Sue Birdseye, *When Happily Ever After Shatters* (Carol Stream, Ilinois: Tyndale House Publishers, Inc., 2013), p. 5.

[vii] II Chronicles 20:15, 17 (New International Version)

[viii] Kari West, Noelle Quinn, *When He Leaves* (Eugene, OR: Harvest House, 1998), p. 103.

[ix] Genesis 12:1-3, (New International Version)

142

[x] Psalm 13:1-2, (New King James Version)

[xi] Psalm 13:5-6, (New King James Version)

[xii] Angela Thomas, *My Single Mom Life* (Nashville, TN: Thomas Nelson, 2007), p. 168.

[xiii] Corrie Ten Boom, Elizabeth and John Sherrill, *The Hiding Place* (Grand Rapids, MI: Chosen Books, 2006), p. 42.

[xiv] West, Quinn, *When He Leaves,* p. 217.

[xv] Ibid., p. 163.

[xvi] Ibid., p. 254.

[xvii] Catherine Claire Larson, *As* We Forgive, (Grand Rapids, MI: Zondervan, 2009), p. 88.

[xviii] Pete Wilson, *Plan B* (Nashville, TN: Thomas Nelson, 2009), p. 96.

[xix] Galatians 5:1, (New International Version)

[xx] Isaiah 55:9, (New International Version)

[xxi] "Brennan Manning Live at Woodcrest," from Woodcrest Church, Columbia, MO, posted by "toddster5," May 30, 2007, www.youtube.com/watch?v=pQi_IDV2bgM.

[xxii] Ephesians 4:26, (New International Version)

[xxiii] Psalms 45:13 (New King James Version)

[xxiv] Andy Stanley, *Guardrails Avoiding Regrets in Your Life* (Grand Rapids, MI: Zondervan, 2011), p. 34.

[xxv] Bethany Haley Williams, PhD, *The Color Of* Grace (New York, NY: Howard Books, 2015), p. 286.

[xxvi] Kara Tippets, Jill Lynn Buteyn, *Just Show Up*, (Colorado Springs, CO: David C Cook, 2015), p. 65.

[xxvii] Mark Nepo, *The Exquisite Risk (New York, NY: Three Rivers, 2005), p.5.*

[xxviii] Curt Thompson, *Ana*tomy of the Soul, (Carol Stream, IL: Tydale, 2010), p. xiv.

[xxix] Proverbs 3:13 (New International Version)

[xxx] James 1:5 (New International Version)

[xxxi] Proverbs 4:6-7 (New International Version)

[xxxii] Elisabeth Elliot, (n.d). AZQuotes.com. Retrieved May 06, 2017, from AZQuotes.com Web site: http://www.azquotes.com/quote/408981

[xxxiii] Kara Tippets, Jill Lynn Butelyn, *Just Show Up*, (Colorado Springs, CO: David C Cook, 2015), p. 18.

[xxxiv] I Corinthians 12:27 (New International Version)

Made in the USA
Middletown, DE
04 October 2021